31 EMAIL HACKS THAT GET A FASTER RESPONSE

Includes 50 samples to use now

Paula Peters

Copyright © 2020 Paula Peters

All rights reserved

The characters and events portrayed in this book are fictitious. Any similarity to real persons, living or dead, is coincidental and not intended by the author.

No part of this book may be reproduced, or stored in a retrieval system, or transmitted in any form or by any means, electronic, mechanical, photocopying, recording, or otherwise, without express written permission of the publisher.

Cover design by: Karla Snider, Clear Marketing Design
ISBN: 9798665005768
Printed in the United States of America

To my clients, friends, family, and class participants:

I hope this book helps take your writing (and career) to the "next level."

I love sharing new writing tricks and hacks with you!

CONTENTS

Title Page
Copyright
Dedication
Having Trouble Getting Replies to Your Emails?
You Can Read This Book in 10 Minutes or Less

Today's Reader Has ZERO Time—and ZERO Patience	1
9 Common Mistakes People Make in Email	6
Don't Write Emails…the Way You Learned in High School	11
NOW…Get FASTER Replies to Emails	15
PAULA'S EMAIL STRATEGY #1—Stick to 2 Paragraphs, 2 Sentences Each	16
PAULA'S EMAIL STRATEGY #2—Ask a Question in the Subject Line	19
PAULA'S EMAIL STRATEGY #3—Try Multiple Choice	21
PAULA'S EMAIL STRATEGY #4—Suggest a Timeframe for Response	26
PAULA'S EMAIL STRATEGY #5—Answer the "WHY?" First	28
PAULA'S EMAIL STRATEGY #6—Ask for Action Upfront	30
PAULA'S EMAIL STRATEGY #7—Lower the Reading Level	33
PAULA'S EMAIL STRATEGY #8—Use the SHORTEST Sentences Possible	37

PAULA'S EMAIL STRATEGY #9—Push Pleasantries to the Bottom of the Email	41
PAULA'S EMAIL STRATEGY #10—Personalize the Subject Line with the Reader's Name	43
PAULA'S EMAIL STRATEGY #11—Bold the Key Points	45
PAULA'S EMAIL STRATEGY #12—Try Subheaders	48
PAULA'S EMAIL STRATEGY #13—Use Bullets Whenever Possible	52
PAULA'S EMAIL STRATEGY #14—Create a Professional Signature Block	55
PAULA'S EMAIL STRATEGY #15—Try an "Em Dash"	58
PAULA'S EMAIL STRATEGY #16—Stick to 1 Topic (or Question)	61
PAULA'S EMAIL STRATEGY #17—Use the Casual Narrative Voice	64
PAULA'S EMAIL STRATEGY #18—Be Positive!	67
PAULA'S EMAIL STRATEGY #19—Don't cc: Too Many People	70
PAULA'S EMAIL STRATEGY #20—DON'T SHOUT IN YOUR EMAIL!	72
PAULA'S EMAIL STRATEGY #21—Use Acronyms	74
PAULA'S EMAIL STRATEGY #22—Shorten Words Whenever Possible	77
PAULA'S EMAIL STRATEGY #23—Use Numbers (But Don't Spell Them Out)	79
PAULA'S EMAIL STRATEGY #24—Add Emojis	81
PAULA'S EMAIL STRATEGY #25—Use a Casual Greeting	84
PAULA'S EMAIL STRATEGY #26—Skip the Formal Closing	86
PAULA'S EMAIL STRATEGY #27—Be Careful with Attachments	88

PAULA'S EMAIL STRATEGY #28—Add an Exclamation Point!	91
PAULA'S EMAIL STRATEGY #29—Send the Email to Yourself First	93
PAULA'S EMAIL STRATEGY #30—Change the Subject Line on Replies and Forwards	95
PAULA'S EMAIL STRATEGY #31—Stop the CYA Madness	97
BONUS STRATEGY #1—New Email Trends	99
BONUS STRATEGY #2—Emailing a Conservative Audience	102
12 Examples of BAD EMAILS—DON'T Steal These!	106
50 Examples of GOOD EMAILS—PLEASE Steal These!	112
Sources	133
Notes	135
Acknowledgements	139
About The Author	141
Books By This Author	143

HAVING TROUBLE GETTING REPLIES TO YOUR EMAILS?

D o you have these email issues?
- Don't get a response to your emails
- Need urgent replies
- Can't get your boss to answer questions in email
- Don't hear back from customers
- Don't get a reply from recruiters

If so, it probably isn't your fault. People today spend only 11.1 seconds reading an email—and the average American office worker receives 200+ emails every single day. That's a LOT of email!!

But there are writing tricks for getting around these roadblocks of time and attention. And they're actually pretty easy.

I am a technical writer who writes emails to the world's busiest readers—military generals, Fortune 500 execs, and chiefs of staff. I have tested all of these techniques with my super-busy readers, and they work exceptionally well. I also teach them in my technical and marketing writing classes, and students love them.

Try 1-2 of my hacks in your emails, and see if they work for your audience. At a minimum, I'm hoping they help you get a faster response. Or please, steal some of the 50 professional emails included at the end of this book (just remember to edit the names!).

I'm betting these easy tricks will solve some of your toughest email issues!

YOU CAN READ THIS BOOK IN 10 MINUTES OR LESS

Throughout this book, I've given you a few simple hacks and tricks to make your email very digestible for today's audience. There are also some "new rules" to writing that I'm going to share with you.

You can probably read this book in under 10 minutes—just by reading the headlines. If you need more detail, then go ahead and read the rest of the chapter content.

But you only need to read the headlines to get the main idea of how to change your emails to get a better response. So...go for it!

This book is perfect if you:

- Feel like people don't read your emails
- Need to get answers quickly by email
- Routinely email high-profile customers, executives, or managers
- Do your sales via email
- Are looking for a job—and email recruiters regularly

TODAY'S READER HAS ZERO TIME— AND ZERO PATIENCE

Do you ever have trouble getting someone to read—or respond—to your emails? Don't feel bad, because you're not alone.

In fact, EVERYONE today is having difficulty getting their emails read and responded to. That's because today's audience has zero time, zero patience, and a TON of email to process... every single day.

My name is Paula Peters, and I'm a technical writer. For the last 21 years, I've owned a business writing technical documents (like reports, procedures, training manuals, and e-books) for big organizations all over the globe—like Russell Stover, Applebee's, Lindt & Sprügli, the U.S. Army, U.S. Strategic Command, Sprint, and EDS.

During that time, I've written LOTS of emails—to my clients and team members, but also as a ghostwriter for my clients. Many of them are written to Fortune 500 executives, chiefs of staff, and 1- or 2-star generals or admirals.

And guess what? Even THEY have a tough time getting their emails answered!

I also teach technical writing classes for executives, senior-level military leaders, government agencies, colleges, and large corporations—where I share techniques for how to write documents better, faster, easier.

As I travel across the country every month, I hear the same questions over and over:

- How do I get my boss to answer my emails?
- How can I get a FASTER response to my email?
- How do I get recruiters to answer my emails?
- How can I get customers to answer my emails?
- What's the best way to approach an executive—by email?

The good news is that it's actually not very hard to get an email response today—if you understand the way people now read and write. (But know this: it's very different than how we learned to write in high school or college!)

People Now Spend Only 11.1 Seconds Reading an Email

Guess how much time people spend reading an email today?

Nope, it's not 2 minutes, or 60 seconds, or even 30 seconds. According to Salesforce.com, people spend an average of **only 11.1 seconds** reading an email today.[1] That's not a lot of time to get your message across![*]

Why do we all spend so little time reading emails? Because we all receive SO MANY EMAILS, every single day.

In fact, *Forbes* magazine recently reported that the average office worker in the U.S. **receives 200 emails/day**—and writes an average of 40 emails/day.[2]

Wow...that's a lotta email!

Think About Your Audience—

Before You Click "SEND"

Before you click "Send," I really want you to think about your audience:

- Who will read this email?
- How much time will they spend reading it?
- Where will they read it? (subway, home, work, car...?)
- What type of device will they read it on? (laptop, tablet, smartphone, desktop PC...?)

The lesson here is simple: make your email short and sweet enough to be read in 11.1 seconds.

A big, lunky, 4-5 paragraph email doesn't cut it for today's audience. If it's not simple enough to be read (and digested) in 11.1 seconds, then it will get skipped over in favor of the next (shorter) one!

Most Emails Today Are Read on a Smartphone

Email has come a long way since it was invented in the 1970s. Today, the average American office worker spends 2.5 hours every single day—just dealing with email.[3]

As the volume of email continues to grow, so do our strategies for how to deal with it. A recent study shows that **61.9% of all emails are now opened on a smartphone**.[4] (And according to another study by Adobe, that number is as high as **88% for millennial email readers**.)[5]

It's also interesting that people now check their email 24/7. In fact, *Forbes* estimates that Americans check their email 15x/day (or more):[6]

50% check email in bed
42% check email in the bathroom

18% check email while driving(!)[7]

What does this have to do with your email? It means that when you send an email, it's very likely that your reader will:

- Read your email on a smartphone or tablet
- NOT read your email on a large desktop monitor (as little as 9.8% of emails are now opened on a desktop)[8]
- Have very little time to read it, digest it, and think of a response
- Only choose 40 emails to reply to today[9]

The Struggle Is Real: the Daily Tsunami of Email

It is very difficult to read 200+ emails every day. Time and again, when I teach my technical writing classes at sites all over the U.S., my participants complain about being swamped by email.

It doesn't matter if they are desk clerks, customer service reps, technicians, managers, or 4-star generals. I call it the "tsunami of email"—because everyone is drowning in an overwhelming wave of daily email.

And that tsunami repeats every morning, as soon as they turn on their device: smartphone, laptop, tablet, or desktop.

As a result, many office workers now answer email around the clock, so they don't get flooded by the tidal wave in the morning.

Know How People Read Email Today

If you want to be one of the 40 emails (out of 200) that gets answered by your reader today, then you need to understand the "survival strategies" people use to cope with the daily onslaught of email.

Here's how people process email today:

1. **Delete unimportant emails**—to whittle down their task.
2. **Answer important emails first**—such as from their boss, a client, or an executive.
3. **Answer easy emails next**—bang out 2-3 quick replies before starting their meeting.
4. **Finally, read 1 more complicated email**—if they have extra time.

Another strategy? Using the "preview window" in their email app—which shows the first 1-2 lines of the email.

This allows them to read the email without actually opening it. By doing that, they can judge whether the email is too long (or complicated) to spend time on.

The Good News...

The goal is to get into the 40+ emails that actually receive a response today from your reader.

The good news is this: it's not as hard as you think, once you understand how writing and reading strategies have changed over the last 10 years.

Are you ready for a few easy hacks—to penetrate your reader's tsunami of daily email?

9 COMMON MISTAKES PEOPLE MAKE IN EMAIL

About a year ago, I had a 2-star admiral in my class who said, "I've been emailing the White House for weeks on a very important topic, and I can't get an answer. How do I get them to answer my emails?"

People come to my classes all the time to share very well-written emails that have never received a response.

"This is a really important topic!" they tell me. "Why won't (s)he answer my email?"

And they are right—it IS a very important topic, and it usually IS a very important email. The challenge today is:

- **How do I get a response to my email?**

Often, it's because the writer is violating one of the guidelines described below. The email may simply look too long, complicated, or ugly to be digested in 11.1 seconds.

You've probably seen an email like that before. Heck, you've probably **written** an email like that before. I know I have!

Of course, 10 years ago people had the time, patience, and energy to read long and complicated emails...when they were only receiving 6 or 8 emails per day. But today, the volume is much higher.

So if you're having trouble getting responses to your emails (from co-workers, your boss, executives, recruiters, customers), then you might be making one of these mistakes.

Here are the most common issues I see in emails from class participants or clients—or even from other professional writers who contact me for job opportunities:

Mistake #1—Your Email Is Too Long.

The maximum length of an email that can easily be read in 11.1 seconds is about 4 sentences. That equals 2 paragraphs, with 2 sentences in each paragraph.

For super-busy executives, however, I usually stick to 2 sentences TOTAL.

Mistake #2—Your Email Is Too Complicated.

If you want someone to actually respond to your email, your best bet is to make it as simple as possible. Stick to 1 topic. Focus on getting just 1 issue resolved.

If you overwhelm the reader with too many issues, then you'll run the risk of getting no answer at all.

For today's busy audience, it's better to write a second email for a second topic. Narrow focus helps.

Mistake #3—The Reading Level Is Too High.

I routinely receive emails written at a 16th or 18th grade reading level—which is way too high to be read in 11.1 seconds at a stoplight (that's master's degree level!). Know what I mean?

Your target reading level for writing email (even for senior-level executives) is around 3rd or 4th grade (more on that later).

Mistake #4—Your "Chunks" Are Too Big.

Don't be "that guy" who's writing dense, 5-paragraph emails with l-o-n-g sentences that wrap across 3 lines. No one will read that email!

For email, use the shortest possible sentences and paragraphs. The shorter, the better. 2 short paragraphs (with 2 short sentences in each) is plenty.

Mistake #5—You Dumped a Problem in Someone's Lap.

Don't email your boss and say, "I tried doing XYZ, but it didn't work. What should I do now?"

Instead, state the problem (in 1 sentence), then offer a multiple-choice solution (in 2-3 bullets), or recommend a single solution (1 sentence).

Mistake #6—It's Too Big for a Smartphone Screen.

Remember the study we discussed earlier: 61.9% of all emails are now opened on a smartphone.[10] (And according to the additional study we mentioned by Adobe, that number is as high as 88% for millennial readers.)[11]

Don't make your reader scroll through a long message on their Android or iPhone. They won't do it. Instead, visualize how your text will look on a tiny smartphone screen (or better yet, test it out by emailing it to a smartphone—one of my hacks discussed later in this book).

Mistake #7—You Asked Too Many Questions.

Have you ever sent an email to someone with 2 or 3 questions in it? Then noticed that they only answered the first question?

If that's the case, then you're asking to many questions. Ask 1 question per email. If you need to ask a second question, send it in a separate email.

Mistake #8—You Didn't Answer the Question, "Why Should I Read This Email?"

If you can't tell the reader WHY the email justifies 11.1 seconds of their day, then you may not get a response.

Your reader opens every email thinking: "Why is this topic important to ME? Why should I spend 11.1 seconds on it? Why do I care?"

The better you relate the email to their needs, values, concerns —the more likely you are to get a response.

Mistake #9—You Wrote It the Way You Learned in High School or College.

Today's reader is accustomed to extremely short Instagram posts, TikTok videos, YouTube videos, hashtags, and tweets. When you write the way you learned in school, it reads like Shakespeare.

Skip the fancy language and get right to the point—using the most casual language possible.

DON'T WRITE EMAILS...THE WAY YOU LEARNED IN HIGH SCHOOL

Let's talk about that last point a little more. When you and I were in high school and college, we learned a very specific style of writing: long, academic sentences... using the biggest words possible.

Unfortunately, people don't read that way anymore. What happened?

Technology Has Changed How We Write

I started to see an incredible revolution in the documents I wrote for my clients around 12 years ago. And little by little, year over year, that revolution has grown.

Interestingly, that's not long after Apple launched the first iPhone, in 2007.[12]

Then the iPad was launched in 2010[13] (and smartphones became more widespread in general), and new apps started making small changes to how we write and read things.

It began with rich texting and emojis—then evolved to Facebook, Twitter, Snapchat, Instagram, TikTok.

Eventually, over 10-15 years, these tiny changes have cumulated into a giant "sea change" of how we write things, a revolution that has slowly bled into our workplace (especially in emails).

As a result of this new technology, most people today prefer reading short, simple, fast, friendly sentences—rather than the long, academic sentences we learned in school.

Why? Because those short sentences are more efficient.

We've basically rewired our brains to process content faster than ever—thanks to a decade of speed-reading texts, tweets, posts, and snaps.

But unfortunately, many schools still teach the l-o-n-g academic sentences of 30 years ago.[†]

The Subject Line Is THE Most Important Line of Your Email

There is only 1 line of your email that I can GUARANTEE will get seen by the reader: the subject line. That's because it's the first line of text that pops up in your reader's inbox.

In fact, the subject line is so important that I spend more time editing the subject line of an important email—than I spend writing the entire body of that same email.

A good subject line will:

- Help the reader choose your email
- Tell the reader why the topic is important
- Ask a question
- Request action
- Convey urgency

It's also good to know also that most business folks use their email "preview window" to preview the first line of text in each email. This gives them a quick idea of whether the email will be easy (or difficult) to read and answer, and whether it's worth their time.

A good subject line—with short, clear, direct content—is much more likely to get a response from today's busy reader. So... choose your words carefully!

I like short subject lines because they ensure that the entire sentence easily fits into a smartphone window. Using a question (or a direct request for action) is always a good strategy, too.

According to a recent analysis of 260 million emails by ShowMeLeads, subject lines with 6-10 words have the highest open rates (21%).[14] A separate study of 40 million emails by Boomerang found that 3-4 word subject lines receive the most responses.[15]

In other words, the shorter the subject line—the better. And less than 10 words is ideal.

For example, instead of:

> **SUBJECT: Can you meet our team at Grinder's Bar & Grill—on Tuesday at 10:00 am?**

I would probably use:

> **SUBJECT: Team mtg—Tues. @ 10:00 am at Grinder's?**

But don't be afraid to experiment with longer subject lines. Sometimes, they work great too. Try a couple different approaches to see what works best with your unique audience.

Don't Be Mysterious or Vague in Your Subject Line

What you DON'T want to do is be cute or vague to "grab" the

reader's attention.

A mysterious 1- or 2-word subject line is worse than one that's too long—and can really drive people crazy.

> **SUBJECT: Meeting**
>
> **SUBJECT: Hey**
>
> **SUBJECT: Stuff**
>
> **SUBJECT: Call me!**

Now the reader must guess your topic, and they're already annoyed before they even open it. Or worse, they're left wondering, "Huh?"

Better for you to put too much info into your subject line than too little. And don't waste your time trying to be cute.

Don't Mark Your Email "URGENT"

Likewise, it's very annoying to read a business email today that's marked "urgent" in the subject line with a red exclamation point, to show "high priority." Today's reader wants to make that decision themselves.

If you're discussing an urgent topic, or you have an important question, you can show urgency by adding a timeline for response (see Paula's Email Strategy #4).

NOW...GET FASTER REPLIES TO EMAILS

I've been testing these 31 email hacks for years with my busiest clients—the 2-star generals, chief executive officers, vice presidents, deputies, and chiefs of staff who routinely receive 300, 500, or even 700+ emails/day.

I'm going to share with you the most effective strategies I've found to get an actual response to my emails. Whenever I teach these in my classes, my participants get very excited—and often email me later to share the good results they've received.

Feel free to tweak, modify, steal, borrow, or reinvent these strategies for your specific audience or reader—to see what works best for you. And if you discover a new one you really like, I'd love to hear it! You can reach me at paula@peterswriting.com, or at www.peterswriting.com.

PAULA'S EMAIL STRATEGY #1—STICK TO 2 PARAGRAPHS, 2 SENTENCES EACH

For today's busy reader who receives as many as 200 email messages every day (according to *Forbes*)[16], you'll want to keep your emails as short as possible.

In fact, Boomerang reports that the ideal length for an email is 50-125 words[17]—which is about 4 sentences. Emails longer than 125 words show a declining open rate.[18] In other words, the longer the email (above 125 words), the fewer people will actually read it.

Gone are the days when you could send your boss an 8-paragraph email detailing a long, complicated question or issue. Today's time-challenged managers groan when they receive an email that scrolls to the next screen (and believe me, I've interviewed many senior executives and military leaders about this very issue).

In fact, long emails can actually make readers angry—which is the **opposite** of what you are trying to achieve.

One military deputy chief of staff who attended my class showed me a printout of a 2-page email he received with at least 10 paragraphs.

He was clearly frustrated, and said, "I asked my staff member to rewrite this email. So he sent me back this." He then showed me a slightly shorter version—at 6 paragraphs. "No one has time to read this!"

Don't be THAT GUY who writes 10-paragraph emails. Make them shorter—much shorter—and you'll find that you'll get a better response, faster.

Use 4 Sentences, MAX

The guideline I use in my emails is 4 sentences MAX in the body of the message (not including subject line, salutation, or signature block).

This comes out to 2 paragraphs—with 2 sentences in each paragraph.

Any more than that, and it's difficult to capture the attention of today's audience.

For Busy Executives—Use 2 Sentences TOTAL

It sounds impossible, but it's not. 2 sentences is definitely a very short email! But I get a much better response from busy executives when my email is only 2 lines (or less).

Use your subject line wisely and get straight to the point. Ask for action immediately—and keep the pleasantries to a bare minimum.

Believe me, most executives today are not offended by a short email. In fact, they are usually grateful that you're respecting their time.

What if You MUST Use

Longer Chunks?

Technical writers like me often call paragraphs "chunks" of information. The shorter and simpler your chunks are, the better odds you'll get a response to your email.

If you absolutely MUST use more than 4 sentences in your email, then keep the paragraphs as short as possible.

Don't use more than 1-2 sentences in a paragraph. This makes it easier to read on a smartphone or tablet. (No more 5-sentence paragraphs, please!)

Add a hard space between each chunk, and you're good to go.

Even 1 Sentence Is OK!

The shorter the email, the better. I've sent plenty of 1-sentence emails (usually a question) that get great results.

In fact, this length of email is perfect if you think the email will be viewed on a small device—such as an older iPhone.

The trick here? Use your subject line wisely. That way, you effectively create a 2-line email—even when the body content has only 1 line of text.

Good Example

Here's a good example of a short, effective email. Notice how I used the subject line as an "extra" line of text:

> **SUBJECT: Interested in rescheduling lunch?**
>
> Hi Fred,
>
> Maybe we could meet again Fri. at 11:30 am—at that little Italian bistro on 39th St.?
>
> Paula

PAULA'S EMAIL STRATEGY #2—ASK A QUESTION IN THE SUBJECT LINE

The most important line of any document is the first line. It's the one line I can guarantee you will get read by your audience.

And what is the first line of an email? The subject line.

When you ask a question in the subject line, you'll have a much better chance of getting an answer. Why? Because the reader instantly knows what you need from them—before they even open the email, while they're still scanning their inbox.

Emails that start with questions in the subject line are clearer, simpler, and easier to answer.

For example, compare these 2 email subject lines:

SUBJECT: Taxes
SUBJECT: Can you do my taxes again this year?

Which of these emails looks easier/faster to answer? Which would you answer first, if they both appeared in your inbox? You would probably answer the second email.

Try the question trick and see if it works for you.

But don't make the mistake of asking a question in the subject line—then overwhelming the reader with too much body content in the email. That can still kill your chances of getting a response.

Keep the overall body of the email short and sweet, with no more than 2-4 sentences total.

Also, keep the question fairly short—the shorter, the better (no more than 5-10 words, MAX). And feel free to use abbreviations, numerals, or acronyms in your subject line!

Good Subject Line Questions

Here are a few great examples of subject lines that I've used (or seen) over the years:

    SUBJECT: Can you approve this by 3:00 pm?
    SUBJECT: Landon, does this work—for the Cerner proposal?
    SUBJECT: What did you decide—about hiring XYZ?
    SUBJECT: Can we try this?
    SUBJECT: Schedule a meeting for Fri.?
    SUBJECT: Are we still "on"—for Tues. 10:30 am?
    SUBJECT: Want to receive your 2023 benefits?
    SUBJECT: Did you review the Q4 finances yet?

PAULA'S EMAIL STRATEGY #3—TRY MULTIPLE CHOICE

When you need a quick answer from a busy boss or executive, try giving them multiple choice in your email.

Sounds easy, doesn't it? Well...it is!

Simply state the problem you're having (1 sentence), then ask how the executive would like to proceed (1 sentence). Then offer 2-3 choices of solutions (labeled A, B, C—or #1, #2, #3).

Good Example

SUBJECT: Broken copier?

Hi Allison,

The new copy machine is broken—and we're unable to prep copies for the Nelson trial. What would you like to do?

    A. Call a repairman from ProCopy Systems
    B. Borrow the copier from the 3rd floor—just to prep for trial
    C. Order a new copier—from OfficeMax

Paula

By making your email easy to answer (and giving a few options), you'll get a faster response.

Don't be surprised (or offended) if you receive a super-short response. It might even be a single word!

For example, Allison may email you back:

> **SUBJECT: Broken copier?**
>
> B works – then we'll buy a new one after Jan. 1.
>
> Thanks!
>
> Allison

Or she may simply reply:

> **SUBJECT: Broken copier?**
>
> Option B.
>
> Allison

That's totally fine! Remember, your boss is being drowned by a daily tsunami of email—and you made it fast and easy for her to answer your email. Goal accomplished!

To make this email even simpler, be sure to prompt your reader with a question in the subject line—like I did above. Play around with the multiple-choice/question-subject combo to see what works best with your specific boss or co-workers.

What if You Already Know Which Action Your Boss Should Take?

If you already know the best solution—but you just need approval to proceed—then do this:

- State the problem (1 sentence)
- Ask for permission to proceed (1 sentence)

- Recommend the best course of action (1 bullet)

This saves your boss even more time—and makes it even EASIER to answer your email quickly.

Good Example

SUBJECT: Can I call a repair man?

Hi Allison,

The new copy machine is broken—and the Nelson trial starts on Monday. Could I:

- Call a repairman from ProCopy Systems?

Let me know if that works for you. Thanks!

Paula

Don't Be Offended by a Short Reply

Once again, don't be surprised or offended if you receive a short, 1-word (or even 1-letter) answer from a busy boss or executive. Remember that your boss is doing their best to answer all the questions and emergencies they receive daily.

But "Y" or "K" is all you need to proceed—and if the answer is "N," at least you know that you probably need a 1-on-1 conversation for clarification.

In this example, Allison might reply:

SUBJECT: Can I call a repair man?

Y

Allison

Don't Dump a Problem in

a Manager's Lap!

The one thing you don't want to do is to just "drop a bomb" in a manager's lap. For example, don't do this:

Bad Example

SUBJECT: HELP??

Hi Allison,

The new copier is broken—and the Nelson trial starts on Monday. What should we do?? Help!!

Paula

Why? Because very few managers today are willing to spend 10 min. typing step-by-step instructions on what to do next. That reply is too complicated to write quickly, so the email sometimes gets put aside—and forgotten.

You'll have better luck getting a response if you proactively offer suggestions or solutions to solve the problem.

What if Your Boss Doesn't Like Your Solution?

No worries. If the boss doesn't like your idea, then they can always pitch another idea to you—which is fine.

Instead of "Y," they might say something like:

SUBJECT: Can I call a repair man?

Let's just buy a new copier at OfficeMax. Use your corporate credit card.

Thanks!

Allison

Great! That's exactly the direction you needed. And even though it wasn't the solution you suggested, you got the conversation started—and received a quick reply to your email.

PAULA'S EMAIL STRATEGY #4 —SUGGEST A TIMEFRAME FOR RESPONSE

Want to create urgency in your email? Simply suggest a timeframe for replying.

Timeframes help readers prioritize emergencies in their inbox. It lets them know that quick action is required.

And by combining a good timeline and a strong "why," we can create urgency—in a polite, non-intrusive way.

Good Example

SUBJECT: Submit lunch order by 9:30 am?

Hi Jules,

Could you submit the lunch order by 9:30 am? Our meeting starts with the client in the Sky Room @ 1:00 pm—and the catering service needs a 3-hr. heads-up.

Thanks for your help!

Paula

Notice that we also included the timeline in the subject. This gives the reader a heads-up on urgency while she's scanning through her inbox.

This strategy works much better (and is less annoying) than marking the email "urgent" using a "!" symbol. It's also less intrusive than saying URGENT in the subject line:

Bad Example

! SUBJECT: URGENT—need lunch for meeting NOW

Hi Jules,

URGENT—we need the lunch order submitted NOW. Our meeting starts with the client @ 1:00 pm in the Sky Room. The cutoff time is 3-4 hrs. before.

Thanks!

Paula

Do you see how much more annoying that second email is? If you have an urgent issue, it's better to use a soft-sell "why," along with a timeline, to get a quick answer.

Examples of Timeframes in Emails

There are many ways you can cite a timeframe (or deadline) in an email, such as:

- Monday morning
- June 5th
- 9/8
- COB tomorrow
- By 1:30 pm

When a busy co-worker is juggling 6 or 7 different tasks in their brain, you can make your request a priority—by stating the timeline clearly upfront. Try it!

PAULA'S EMAIL STRATEGY #5 —ANSWER THE "WHY?" FIRST

When you write an email to someone, you're asking them to spend some of their valuable time reading your words—instead of doing another equally important task. That task could be doing sales, helping customers, or writing that report their boss is waiting for.

So it's important to let them know upfront WHY your email is important.

When your reader opens their inbox in the morning and sees 200 new emails waiting, they're trying to decide which emails to open first. They're asking themselves:

- WHY is this important to me?
- WHO is sending it?
- WHY should I spend 11.1 seconds on this?
- WHY should I choose this email—vs. the other 199 emails?

If you really want to capture the attention of your reader, answer the "why" clearly upfront in the first line of the email (or better yet, in the subject line). That way, you establish immediately that your topic is important—and increase the chances that you'll get a response.

Good Example

SUBJECT: Your healthcare benefits expire Dec. 1

Hi David,

Just a reminder—you will lose your healthcare benefits for next year if you don't complete your registration by 11:59 pm on Dec. 1st.

Please click the link below to register. Thank you!

Paula

Bad Example

SUBJECT: Healthcare benefits

Dear David,

Click the link below for your benefits. Thanks!

Paula

The sooner you answer the question of "why," the more likely that your email will get opened—and that your reader will take action.

PAULA'S EMAIL STRATEGY #6—ASK FOR ACTION UPFRONT

If you need the reader to take action, then request it upfront—in the first line of the email.

Your reader wants to know exactly what you need from them as quickly as possible, without digesting a long, complicated email to get to the bottom line.

Another bonus? You will help make the process easier for the readers who now open 61.9% of their emails on a smartphone.[19] (And remember, that's 88% of all emails, when read by millennials.)[20]

Also, very few readers actually scroll down to the bottom of an email on a smartphone. When they need to, it causes frustration.

If your reader can immediately see what you need when they first open their tiny smartphone screen, they are more likely to answer your message quickly—and they'll appreciate the fact that you got right to the point.

Ask for Action in the Subject Line

Better yet—ask for action directly in the subject line. Then the reader doesn't have to open the email to know what you need.

I use this trick all the time with super-busy executives and military leaders when I need a quick review (or approval) of a document or proposal.

For example, check out these 2 emails. Which grabs your attention first—if you're scrolling through your email inbox?

Bad Example

SUBJECT: Expense reports

Hi Nico,

Here are the 3 expense reports from the Dallas trip. It would be great if you could get to these as soon as possible. That way, employees can receive their checks before mandatory shutdown.

Thanks!

Paula

Good Example

SUBJECT: Approve expense reports by COB Friday?

Hi Nico,

Could you please approve the 3 attached expense reports from the Dallas trip by COB on Friday? Then employees can receive their checks before mandatory shutdown on the 15th.

Thanks!

Paula

What if It's REALLY URGENT?

The best way to convey urgency is to request an action and give a timeline at the same time. You can even softly suggest a consequence if it doesn't happen (just be careful not to sound too "heavy-handed"!).

That's a much better approach than writing "URGENT" in the subject line or marking the email as priority with a red exclamation point "!". Let the reader decide for themselves if the email is urgent—by the deadline, request for action, or possible consequences.

If we revise the above email to suggest a consequence, it might read:

Good Example

SUBJECT: Approve expense reports by COB Friday?

Hi Nico,

Could you please approve the 3 attached expense reports from the Dallas trip by COB on Friday? Then employees can receive their checks before mandatory shutdown on the 15th.

If we don't approve them by COB Friday, they will not receive their reimbursement checks until next year—and I know how grouchy people get about that at Christmas time!

Thanks!

Paula

PAULA'S EMAIL STRATEGY #7 —LOWER THE READING LEVEL

It may seem counterintuitive, but for today's super-busy, highly educated reading audience—you actually need to LOWER the reading level in your email.

In their study of 40 million emails, Boomerang found that emails written at a third-grade reading level got the best response—in fact, they got a 17% better response than those written at a high school reading level, and a whopping 36% better response than those written at a college reading level.[21]

Why? Because it's much faster and easier to read a document written at an elementary-grade reading level than a college-grade reading level.

Reading grade 14 content is S-L-O-W. (Have you ever tried reading a master's thesis? That's what we're talking about here!)

This doesn't mean that we're "dumbing down" the content (a concern many people have when I teach this topic in my writing classes). Not at all.

In fact, American adults have now reached the highest general educational level since data collection began in 1940, according to the U.S. Census Bureau—with 33% of Americans now attaining a bachelor's degree or higher, compared to only 5% in 1940.[22] And 88% of adults in the U.S. today have completed high school (compared to only 25% in 1940).[23]

But although the working population is now more educated, it's still very difficult to read grade 14 content in the 11.1 second timespan that people have available for a single email.

The slower (and more complicated) your email is, the less likely you'll receive a response.

And the funny thing is, most people that I talk to in my classes DON'T REALIZE that they're writing at a grade 14 (or grade 18, or grade 20) reading level. They THINK they're writing much lower, and they want to appear as intelligent as possible in their emails. So the grade level keeps creeping up.

I see this happen all the time—in emails, reports, sales presentations, blogs, and white papers.

How Do You Know if Your Reading Level Is Too High?

Many word processing and email programs today have an option called "Readability Statistics" or "Flesch-Kincaid grade level test" in their proofing options (including Microsoft Word).

By selecting this option in Microsoft Word, for example, the software will test your content for approximate reading level and display the results—after you run a spellcheck.

If it's an important email, I sometimes copy and paste the content into a blank document in Microsoft Word to check the grade level before clicking "Send."

Example—Reading Level Too High

Still don't believe me? Here's an example of 2 emails. One has a high reading level, while the other one has a much lower reading level.

Which of these emails would YOU rather read?

Bad Example—High Reading Level

SUBJECT: Request for training proposal

Good afternoon, Ms. Peters!

We are populating our first quarter of the fiscal year, and your technical writing courses are vital to our continued success. We would like to host you in September for 3 days of your technical writing training, titled "7 Professional Writing Secrets—to Write Better, Faster, Easier," structured as such:

- Day 1 – 8-hour course
- Day 2 – 8-hour course (for a targeted group)
- Day 3 – 1-hour course (designated for strategic executives)

We are continuing with selection for other quarters in the upcoming fiscal year, but right now, we want to inquire into your availability to conduct this course (ideally September). We'd like to engage in the near future for additional sessions throughout the year.

As you know from past collaboration, scheduling can often be our first hurdle. Given the level of these training events, we have several considerations on our end and realize that you have a very busy schedule as well.

We appreciate you working with us and look forward to continuing our relationship with you!

Very respectfully,

Michael

Good Example—Low Reading Level

SUBJECT: Training in September?

Hi Paula,

We're scheduling a few classes for next year…and we'd love for you to teach your popular writing class, "7 Professional Writing Secrets—to Write Better, Faster, Easier," in September!

Do you have any dates available for the following?

- Day 1 – 8-hour course
- Day 2 – 8-hour course (for one single group)
- Day 3 – 1-hour course (a few specific executives)

We're still looking at other dates to bring you back for the rest of the year—but first just want to see if you're free in September.

We're pretty busy—and we know you are too!—so the sooner we can get it on the calendar, the better.

You are awesome to work with, and we're excited to see you here again. Thank you so much!

Michael

See what I mean? Most people prefer the second email…including me.

Bottom line is: lower the reading level in your emails to get a better response. Aim for a third-grade reading level.

Even if you don't feel comfortable going that "low" in your reading level, then just try to get it as far below college-level as possible. The lower, the better!

PAULA'S EMAIL STRATEGY #8— USE THE SHORTEST SENTENCES POSSIBLE

Because we want to lower the reading level in our business emails today (see Strategy #7), it's important to use the shortest, simplest sentences possible.

Why? Because you can read a short sentence MUCH faster than a long one. This is especially true on a tiny smartphone—where 61.9% of all emails are now opened[24] (or where 88% of all emails are opened by millennials).[25]

How Long Should Email Sentences Be?

10 years ago, I regularly wrote 30-word sentences for my clients—in emails, reports, or even sales presentations. Heck, I used semicolons to make sentences longer!

However, a 30-word sentence is WAY too long for today's audience.

Now, I use a guideline of 8-12 words per sentence for email (and really, for just about any business document that I now write).

Yes, Sentence Fragments Are OK in Email

Sentence fragments also work great in email. Those are really, really short sentences that may not even have a subject or a verb (for all you grammar nerds out there, like me!).

I often use sentences like:

- That works!
- Great.
- No problem.
- Sure!
- Yep, that's fine.
- It's good.
- Check this out…
- Still waiting on Hailey.
- Sounds good!
- Looking forward to it!

(Contractions Are OK, Too)

Do I use contractions in emails? Yep, all the time—and you can too.

To help make sentences (and overall email length) even shorter, try using:

- It's
- Can't
- Won't
- Shouldn't
- Here's
- Didn't
- Couldn't

Just make sure you're using them correctly in the sentence!

Even #Hashtags Can Now Be Used in Email

Hashtags are a great way to communicate a complex thought very quickly. You've probably seen them on Instagram, Facebook, and Twitter—and lately, I see them used frequently in email.

Hashtags were originally created to link hot news topics on Twitter. You've probably seen hashtags like: #GameOfThrones, #ShareACoke, #VisitKC, #TLDR, or #tbt (#ThrowbackThursday).

But hashtags are now used in text messages, instant messages, and emails to efficiently express a complex mood, concept, or idea. It can be silly, casual, or fun—and it makes your email seem more personal and friendly. For example:

#smile
#TGIF
#FunnyNotFunny
#LoveThis
#SoEmbarrassing
#fun
#amazing
#WishItWasFriday

If you think your reader is too conservative to understand a hashtag in an email, then skip it. It's just an optional personal "touch" you can add to your message.

How to Use a #Hashtag in an Email

If you do decide to use a hashtag, then 1 or 2 is plenty—but you can add up to 5-6, just for fun. Here's a great example of hashtag use in an email:

Good Example

SUBJECT: Birthday today in breakroom

Hey Marty,

Don't forget—there's cake in the breakroom today at 1:15 pm for Julie's birthday. #NeedABreak #Yum #LoveThisJob #NeverEnoughCake

See you there!
Paula

PAULA'S EMAIL STRATEGY #9— PUSH PLEASANTRIES TO THE BOTTOM OF THE EMAIL

Years ago, I taught an email etiquette class where I instructed participants to start off their emails with a pleasant, personalized greeting before getting into the "meat" of their request.

But today's readers are far too busy for this. They open your email in a rush, constantly asking themselves: "What does she want? What does she need? How fast can I answer this?"

To help them get info as quickly as possible—and increase the chances that they'll actually reply to your email—I now push my pleasantries to the very BOTTOM of the email.

That way, I can still be friendly and caring, while also respecting their time.

So ask for action upfront, in the beginning. Then be polite at the end.

To show you the difference, here's an example of an email I wrote years ago:

Bad Example

SUBJECT: Estimate for client project

Dear Karla,

It was great seeing you at lunch yesterday. And I loved the cookies!

By the way—could you please review this project scope, and send me an estimate by 3:00 pm tomorrow? Thanks!

Paula

Good Example

Here's how I would write the same email now, 10 years later:

SUBJECT: Estimate for client project

Hi Karla,

Could you please review this project scope for our client, and send me an estimate by 3:00 pm tomorrow?

By the way, it was great seeing you at lunch yesterday. Loved the cookies!

Thanks,
Paula

Both emails are very polite, but the second one gets right to the point—and has a better chance of getting a response.

PAULA'S EMAIL STRATEGY #10— PERSONALIZE THE SUBJECT LINE WITH THE READER'S NAME

According to Constant Contact, your email open rate increases by 29% when the subject line is personalized with the user's name.[26] That goes for sales emails, marketing emails, and direct business emails to a peer, co-worker, client, or manager. For example:

Good Example

SUBJECT: Anthony, review budget by Thursday?

Obviously, this gets a lot more attention than:

Bad Example

SUBJECT: Budget review

See the difference between these 2 subject lines?

The first one grabs your attention immediately and builds a sense of urgency. (By using a question in the subject line, you also increase that sense of urgency.)

The second email, however, just looks like a run-rate form letter.

Why does this trick work so well? Because as humans, we recognize our own names very quickly. Even if there are hundreds of emails in our inbox, our names pop out immediately.

CAUTION: Don't Overuse the Name Trick!

This trick works very well in my own personal experience, such as when I'm under a tight deadline and need a quick response from a busy executive. But I definitely DO NOT OVERUSE IT.

When you do this too often, it gets annoying for the reader—and even creepy. And by the way, you'll want to stick to first name only.

...And Don't Mention Other Personal Details

Another creepy thing for a reader? When other personal info (besides their first name) is included in the subject line.

As a general guideline, I don't mention anything other than their first name in the subject line—unless it's a personal friend, or unless the info applies directly to the question or topic in the body of the email.

PAULA'S EMAIL STRATEGY #11—BOLD THE KEY POINTS

To make important information stand out in your email —such as meeting times, names, action items, or due dates—it's great if you can highlight key words and phrases in bold.

Don't go crazy with it. You don't want too much bold text! But choosing 1 or 2 phrases in each paragraph makes the email much faster to read, by making key information highly visible.

I've used this little trick to highlight:

- Statistics
- Deadlines
- Facts
- Dollar figures
- Calendar dates
- Names of people
- Action items

Draw Attention to a Deadline

For example, a few bolded words can really draw attention to a deadline. Notice how quickly you are able to read the following email, using the bolded words as a guideline:

Good Example

SUBJECT: Your entry form?

Hi Scott,

Just a reminder—your **entry form** must be received **by June 25th** in order to qualify for the awards program.

Thank you!
Paula

Stand Out from Dense Content

Or maybe you have a very long email, with a lot of dense content—but only 2-3 items really need to stand out. In that case:

Good Example

SUBJECT: Your entry form?

Hi Scott,

Just a reminder—your entry form must be **received by June 25th** in order to qualify for the awards program. There are multiple categories you can submit to. Please choose your **best 3 categories** on your entry form.

In addition, you will be required to submit an attachment for each of your top 3 categories. Be sure to **submit 1 work sample for each of the 3 categories** on your entry form (for a **total of 3 work samples**).

Thank you!
Paula

When You're Sending a

Group Email...Try This

Bold text can also clarify who's responsible for an action in a group email. Try this:

Good Example

SUBJECT: Potluck setup?

Hi Avery and Jessamyn,

Is there any chance you could help us set up the training room for the potluck lunch today? **Jessamyn**—we could use your awesome decorating skills! **Avery**—we'd love to borrow the extra table from your office.

Thanks so much!
Paula

Now Avery and Jessamyn can see their individual action items very quickly—and respond immediately, without wondering who is responsible for what.

PAULA'S EMAIL STRATEGY #12— TRY SUBHEADERS

If you MUST write an email longer than 4 sentences (for example, a 2-page sales proposal, or an email to coordinate a cross-functional meeting), then try using subheaders.

What Is a Subheader?

Subheaders are short subtitles that visually break up the content of a longer document into short "chunks" or sections. They typically use a larger, bold font, and sometimes a color—to offset them from the rest of the text. (Another option: all capital letters.)

Subheaders give a quick visual cue to help readers digest the content of a longer email.

Using a Subheader in Email

An email subheader should be 1-10 words long. Use at least 2-3 subheaders in your email, one above each "chunk" of content.

For example, if you're coordinating a meeting, you sometimes need to include a LOT of information:

Bad Example

SUBJECT: Holiday party planning meeting

Hi Jacob,

Thank you for helping us plan the holiday party! We're all going to meet at 9:30 am on Monday, November 10th in the Ellis Room on the 7th floor. Jessica, Susan, Scott, and Zack will be there too.

I'll be asking you about the projector and screen rental, plus the PowerPoint slides with photos that you talked about running—so don't forget those. Look forward to seeing you there!

Paula

Instead, you can use headers to visually organize the same info:

Good Example

SUBJECT: Holiday party planning meeting

Hi Jacob,

Thanks for helping us plan the holiday party!

DATE/TIME
Monday, November 10th—9:30 am

LOCATION
Ellis Room—7th floor

ATTENDEES
- Jessica
- Susan
- Scott
- Zack
- Jacob
- Paula

ACTION ITEMS
- **Jacob**—projector/screen rental + PowerPoint slides with photos
- **Susan**—food from caterer
- **Zack**—lighting and electrical requirements
- **Jessica**—napkins, plates, forks, serving dishes, etc.

Look forward to seeing you there!

Paula

Types of Subheaders You Can Use

There are a few different types of subheaders you can try using in an email. I use ALL of these on a regular basis. You can:

- Ask a question
- Provide a description
- Use a summary

For example, we can rewrite the meeting coordination email above using question subheaders. It would look like this—and be just as effective:

Good Example

SUBJECT: Holiday party planning meeting

Hi Jacob,

Thank you for helping us plan the holiday party!

When Is the Meeting?
Monday, November 10th—9:30 am

Where Will the Meeting Be Held?
Ellis Room—7th floor

Who Should Attend?
- Jessica

- Susan
- Scott
- Zack
- Jacob
- Paula

What Are Your Action Items?

- **Jacob**—projector/screen rental + PowerPoint slides with photos
- **Susan**—food from caterer
- **Zack**—lighting and electrical requirements
- **Jessica**—napkins, plates, forks, serving dishes, etc.

Look forward to seeing you there!

Paula

How to Format a Subheader

A good email header should stand out from the text. You don't have to go crazy with it. Try using one (or more) of these:

- Bold
- All capital letters
- Small caps
- A single color
- Slightly larger font

In an email or report, I typically use one color from the logo (either mine, or the customer's) with a 14- or 16-point bold font.

(I stay away from underline, italics, or multiple colors. Those techniques look pretty old-fashioned today.)

Just be consistent, and keep your headers the same font, size, and color throughout the email.

PAULA'S EMAIL STRATEGY #13—USE BULLETS WHENEVER POSSIBLE

If you ARE writing a longer email, then in addition to subheaders—you'll want to use bullets.

Bullets are an easy way to lighten up dense content and build some "white space" into your email. This makes it easier to digest quickly.

Bullets also stand out on the page, so the reader's eye goes directly to them.

I use bullets on all types of documents (such as reports, PowerPoint presentations, and training manuals), but I especially use them on emails. It's an easy way to organize lists of items for the reader.

Bad Example

For example, instead of saying:

> Hi Joe,
>
> When you get a minute, we'll need you to please review the attached: prepayment invoice, proposal agreement, and

certificate of insurance. Just sign and return when you are done. Thanks!

Paula

You can really clean up this email by adding a few easy bullets:

Good Example

Hi Joe,

Could you please review the attached when you get a minute?

- Prepayment invoice
- Proposal agreement
- Certificate of insurance

Just sign and return when you are done. Thanks!

Paula

See how much easier it is to read a bullet list, rather than a complex paragraph?

Some Rules About Bullets in Email

When you use bullets in an email, just capitalize the first letter. Skip the punctuation at the end of each bullet.

Also, the following are all OK to use in bullets:

- Single words
- Sentence fragments
- Phrases
- Incomplete sentences

No More Than 5 Bullets, Please!

When adding bullets to an email (or any document), you don't want to use too many. Around 1-5 bullets are plenty.

Any bullet list longer than that will probably get ignored.

You Can Also Try—Just 1 Bullet

I sometimes use just one single bullet to highlight a key point in the email for a super-busy reader. For example, if a client asks me for an estimate, I often send an email like this:

Good Example

> Hi Anthony,
>
> Sure, we can write this article for you on conveyor belts. If this estimate works, just email me approval and we'll start tomorrow:
>
> - **500-word article**—interview contacts, research technical specs, write 1 draft, do 2 rounds of revisions, perform graphic layout, final proofread = $350
>
> Thanks!
>
> Paula

PAULA'S EMAIL STRATEGY #14 —CREATE A PROFESSIONAL SIGNATURE BLOCK

A simple way to establish credibility—and share your contact info—is to use a signature block at the bottom of your message.

What's in a Signature Block?

A good signature block has the following information (you can pick and choose, depending on what best represents you and your organization):

Minimum Info to Include

- Full name
- Phone number
- Email address

You Might Also Want to Include...

- Job title
- Company name
- Company address
- Company logo
- Website (with hyperlink)
- Social networking links or icons (LinkedIn, Twitter, Facebook)
- Link to a GPS map (if location is important, such as for a storefront)

What if You Work for a Big Company?

If you work for a large company, or if you're the franchisee of a large company, then there is probably already a standard signature block that you should use in your emails. (Your company will probably want you to use the standard one—rather than creating your own.)

Not sure what it looks like? Try asking your:

- Boss
- Communications department
- Human resources department
- IT department

When to Use a Signature Block

Once you create your signature block, make sure your email app is set to automatically add it to:

- New messages
- Replies
- Forwarded messages

Do You Need a Signature Block for Personal Emails?

A signature block gives you credibility, and makes you look more professional—even if it's just for personal email. You can use it to apply for jobs, send emails to the electric company, or just share it with friends and family.

Here's my personal signature block. Notice I include a promo at the bottom for my business—and you can do that, too!

Good Example

Paula Peters
Peters Writing Services, Inc.
Ph (913) 485-4537
paula@peterswriting.com

Sign up for my FREE writing tricks + hacks email...2x/year! www.peterswriting.com

PAULA'S EMAIL STRATEGY #15— TRY AN "EM DASH"

The em dash is one of the hot new trends in writing, and it's growing in popularity. It's very versatile, and can replace a comma, colon, semicolon, or even parentheses—and is handy for breaking up a long sentence. (See how I used it there?)

An em dash looks like this: —

It's like a longer hyphen, and it has become more common in casual writing—especially in emails. (Although I'm seeing them used more frequently now in more "formal" writing also, such as reports, web content, and training manuals.)

Bad Example

To show you how it works, let's look at a long sentence from this email:

> Hi Susan,
>
> If you'd prefer to pay by card, then I can send you an email payment link; we accept any type of credit or debit card.
>
> Thanks!
>
> Paula

This is a fairly long sentence for an email. I would probably switch this to an em dash:

Good Example

Hi Susan,

If you'd prefer to pay by card, then I can send you an email payment link—we accept any type of credit or debit card.

Thanks!

Paula

See how much quicker and easier it is to read that LONG sentence?

Bad Example

I also like to use it to replace parentheses. For example, instead of this:

Hi Morgan,

We could meet for lunch on Tues. (or even Wed., Thurs., or Fri.) of next week. Would one of those days work for you?

Looking forward to it!

Paula

Let's rewrite that LONG sentence using an em dash:

Good Example

Hi Morgan,

We could meet for lunch next week—Tues., Wed., Thurs., or Fri. Would one of those work for you?

Looking forward to it!

Paula

I strongly encourage you to try using an em dash in your next email. It's a fast, easy way to make a longer sentence easy to digest.

I use them all the time, even with very conservative audiences!

PAULA'S EMAIL STRATEGY #16— STICK TO 1 TOPIC (OR QUESTION)

I often see people (even execs) make the mistake of squeezing a bunch of topics into a single email, to try to be efficient.

This often backfires when the reader gets overwhelmed by the complexity of the email.

So instead of getting SOME answers, they get NO answers.

I recommend using a guideline of 1 topic (or question) per email. If you have another topic or question to cover, send a second email.

You'll be more likely to get a response to 1 (or both) emails—than if you try to squeeze both things into 1 longer message.

For example, instead of doing this:

Bad Example

SUBJECT: Pick up office supplies?

Hi Taylor,

> Could you swing by and pick up some office supplies on the way to XYZ Company's office? We're out of black ink.
>
> Oh, and by the way—did you have time to put together the agenda for the Tues. meeting? Remember that Aiden will be attending this week. Did you include his action items?
>
> Thanks!
>
> Paula

The first problem is that Taylor may never even see both questions. If she's reading the email on her smartphone (and there's a good chance that she is), then she probably will NOT scroll down to the second paragraph.

She might assume there's only one question, send a quick answer, then close the email. Or she might get overwhelmed by all the questions in both paragraphs, and save the email for later.

The second problem is that if she gets busy later (or receives a bunch of new emails), she may never go back to it.

Instead, try separating these questions into 2 different emails. It may even help to send them a few minutes (or hours) apart.

I often wait for a busy executive or client to answer my first email before sending the second one. That way, I don't overwhelm him or her.

Of course, this requires you to prioritize which question to send first!

Good Example

> **SUBJECT: Pick up office supplies?**
>
> Hi Taylor,
>
> Could you pick up some office supplies today—on the way to XYZ Company's office? We're out of black ink.

Thanks!

Paula

And then, 2 hours later:

Good Example

SUBJECT: Agenda—for Tues. meeting

Hi Taylor,

Forgot to ask—do you have time to put together the agenda for the Tues. meeting?

Remember that Aiden is attending this week, so we'll need his action items also. Thanks (again)!

Paula

PAULA'S EMAIL STRATEGY #17— USE THE CASUAL NARRATIVE VOICE

It's important today to use the most casual, friendly language you possibly can.

The more formal, technical, or academic the language in your email, the less likely anyone will respond to it.

Why is that? Because people today have a healthy distrust of wasting time on anything that looks like a "form letter."

The assumption is that if the email is not personalized to the reader, then it's not important.

It's better to be as personal, friendly, and approachable as possible. You can show respect to your reader today by being considerate of their time—rather than by being rigid and formal, like we did in the 1990s.

How to Use the Casual Narrative Voice in Email

Your emails today should use what I call the "casual narrative voice." This means using the less-formal first or second person

(I, you, we).

It should sound like you are having a casual, face-to-face conversation with the person.

This replaces the older, more antiquated third-person referral to yourself or your own company (it, they). For example:

Bad Example

> It has come to the attention of **this company** that the **above account** is past due. **Account holder** should advise in writing on when this issue will be resolved, and whether **the bank** can provide any assistance in this matter.

Good Example

> **We** just noticed that **your** credit account has missed a couple of payments. Can **you** email **us** and let us know when **we** can expect to receive your next payment? Also, is there anything **we** can do to help **you** resolve this?

The very formal use of "this company" and "the bank" make the first email sound like a form letter...the kiss of death for emails today.

Time and again, I see businesses make the mistake of being WAY too formal for today's audience—and failing to speak in a conversational tone. Use the casual narrative voice as much as possible.

A Few Exceptions to Know About

I still occasionally come across a few organizations and documents that use a more formal narrative voice (although there seem to be less every year).

Here's a few common exceptions to be aware of:

- **Legal documents**—lawyers have been trained to write in formal language and tend to prefer it, even when they move on to other careers. If your boss or customer is (or was) a lawyer, be aware of this.
- **Government**—even though President Obama signed the "Plain Writing Act" into law in 2010 with the goal of making government regulations easier to understand, federal and state agencies still struggle with this.
- **Military**—there are still pockets of the military (and certain departments and bases) that use vastly formal language, although younger officers are slowly changing that.
- **Older forms**—you may be using older, outdated forms or templates with antiquated language.
- **Your old-fashioned boss**—if your boss is just plain formal, then you'll want to follow their lead and mimic their email style, to get a better response from him or her.

PAULA'S EMAIL STRATEGY #18— BE POSITIVE!

A good guideline for writing emails today is to keep the tone as positive and happy as possible. Today's readers are more likely to respond to emails that are upbeat and positive.

In fact, when Boomerang analyzed email response rates, they found that happier emails receive a 15% increase in responses.[27] This means:

- **Be kind**—express to the person how important they are
- **If you're dealing with an issue**—suggest positive solutions upfront
- **If you're waiting for a response**—request action in a positive, friendly manner
- **Don't complain**—use direct, clear requests for action or answers
- **Don't nag**—use timelines to get urgent action accomplished

Nagging Does NOT Work

Today, we show respect (and get a better response) by being positive, happy, and pleasant. For example:

Bad Example

> Hi Brenden,
>
> I'm still waiting for you to give me an update about the Marsten account. I've already sent you 3 emails about this.
>
> Could you get off your butt and do something about this? Please?? This is the third time I've emailed you. We're going to be late on our deadline!
>
> Paula

Let's make this email sound more professional by being positive, happy, and direct. Instead of nagging, we'll create urgency by adding a timeframe and a consequence to boost our chances of getting a response:

Good Example

> Hey Brenden,
>
> I've really enjoyed working with you over the past 6 months on the Marsten account. Would you mind emailing me the final report in Excel—by May 17?
>
> That way, we can still meet our deadline without involving our VP. I know you've been busy, so you probably missed my last couple of emails.
>
> Thank you so much for your awesome work on this project!
>
> Paula

See the difference? The first email places a lot of blame on the reader and is designed to make him respond out of guilt. The second one expresses kindness and focuses on positive action, and gives the reader the benefit of the doubt.

If both of these emails were sent to YOU...which one would

YOU respond to? Probably the second one.

PAULA'S EMAIL STRATEGY #19— DON'T CC: TOO MANY PEOPLE

Gone are the "good old days" of the 1990s and early 2000s when we used to send CYA ("cover your ass") emails to the boss and copy 30 people in the department—including your senior executive.

But today, with the volume of email people are receiving, you're more likely to get a reply if accountability is limited to 1 individual (or 2-3 people, at most).

Don't "Shotgun" Your Email to Tons of People

Now, instead of "shotgunning" your emails to 20 or 30 people, it's much better if you simply direct your question or issue to 1 person (or maybe 2-3 people, max).

(I sometimes even send the exact same email to 2 or 3 different people, rather than copying them all on the same one. I get a better response that way.)

If you DO send the email to 2-3 people, then try addressing each person individually in the email—either in the header, or by bolding to their name.

Then each person can quickly see their specific task, question, or topic. For example:

Bad Example

SUBJECT: Corp taxes due next week

Hi guys,

Corporate taxes are due next week—so we'll need to get all the employee receipts by Thursday, plus the final expense list for Q1-Q4. Thanks!

Paula

There are a couple of things we can do here to help get each reader's attention—and get our issue resolved.

Let's start by adding their names specifically in the greeting, then call out their individual action items.

Good Example

SUBJECT: Corp taxes due next week

Hi Colin and Alexa,

Corporate taxes are due next week. **Colin**—can you send me all the employee receipts by Thursday? And **Alexa**—can you send me the final expense list for Q1-Q4?

Thanks!

Paula

Notice how your eye goes right to the bolded names, making it VERY quick and easy to read. Personalized requests are appreciated because they save time.

PAULA'S EMAIL STRATEGY #20— DON'T SHOUT IN YOUR EMAIL!

I probably don't need to say this, but...you never want to SHOUT in your email (no matter how frustrated you are).

"Shouting" means using all capital letters in a word, phrase, or sentence. For example:

Bad Example

SUBJECT: Budget worksheet

Hi Elizabeth,

I need an electronic copy of the budget worksheet AS SOON AS POSSIBLE. DO YOU UNDERSTAND?

Paula

Doesn't that sound rude? (Your reader will probably think so!)

Instead, create urgency by using a polite question combined with a timeline (and possibly a suggested consequence). This communicates importance—without being offensive.

Here, I would try:

Good Example

SUBJECT: Budget worksheet

Hi Elizabeth,

Could you please send me an electronic copy of the budget worksheet—as soon as you have a moment? We're submitting the final proposal to the Dept. of Defense on Wed.

Thanks!

Paula

The second email is much more polite, much less offensive—and more likely to receive a response from the reader.

PAULA'S EMAIL STRATEGY #21— USE ACRONYMS

It's absolutely OK to use acronyms in email today. In fact, people expect it—especially your more tech-savvy readers. Acronyms shorten emails and save space. Not only that, but they help create a connection with the reader.

Acronyms Build Intimacy with Your Reader

When they're used right, acronyms create a personal connection with your reader, and make your emails more friendly.

Here's an example of a good way to build intimacy, using an acronym:

Good Example

SUBJECT: Thanks for the Q2 report!

Hi Jordan,

BTW...thank you for getting the Q2 report to me so quickly this year. I really appreciate it! (Could end-of-quarter closings get any crazier?? LOL)

Paula

Common Business Acronyms

You can use any common business acronym in an email. I don't even bother defining them—because most people in a business setting will probably know these:

- FY = fiscal year
- Q1 = first quarter
- ASAP = as soon as possible
- BOGO = buy one, get one free
- CEO = chief executive officer
- COB = close of business (for example, today)
- 24/7 = 24 hours per day/7 days per week
- IT = information technology

(Casual Acronyms Are OK, too)

And you don't have to stick to the formal business-related acronyms. I've started using newer, commonly acceptable social media acronyms too, such as:

- LOL = laugh out loud
- IDK = I don't know
- IKR = I know, right?
- IMHO = in my humble opinion
- RN = right now
- BTW = by the way

Make Sure the Reader KNOWS the Acronym...Before You Click "Send"

But before you add an acronym to your email, make sure your reader understands it. You don't want to confuse (or offend) them in any way.

If the acronym is too confusing (or if you're not sure whether they actually know it or not), then skip it.

Don't Use Offensive Acronyms (Unless You REALLY Know Your Reader)!

I personally stay away from any acronyms that might be considered offensive, unless the reader is my mom, brother, or best friend.

And even then, I have sometimes offended them because they can't read my "tone" or mood in the email (especially if I use sarcasm, which is a big no-no in email).

In a business email, I stay away from:

- TLDR = too long, didn't read
- WTF = what the fuck
- WTH = what the hell
- LMAO = laughing my ass off
- LMFAO = laughing my fucking ass off
- AF = as fuck

PAULA'S EMAIL STRATEGY #22— SHORTEN WORDS WHENEVER POSSIBLE

J ust like with acronyms, it's great when you can shorten common business words—to make your emails even shorter, more concise, and more efficient.

Common Shortened Business Words and Symbols

Here are a few of the more common business terms I shorten—even in a "formal" email, or an email to a stranger (such as an executive):

- incl. = include
- mtg. = meeting
- conf. = conference
- proj. = project
- Tues. = Tuesday
- Sept. = September
- approx. = approximately
- est. = estimated
- min. = minutes
- hrs. = hours

- @ = at
- St. = street
- Inc. = incorporated
- "=" = equals

Should You Add a Period to a Shortened Word?

You can add a period at the end, but it doesn't really matter. As punctuation rules get more casual, it is becoming more acceptable to simply use the shortened word itself (for example: "incl" instead of "incl.", or "min" instead of "min.").

Here's an example of an email that uses some common, shortened business terms—without the periods at the end:

Good Example

SUBJECT: Going to year-end meeting?

Hi Debbie,

Are you planning to attend the year-end mtg on Tues? It should run approx 30 min.

Paula

Just make sure your reader understands what the shortened word or symbol means. If in doubt…don't use it!

PAULA'S EMAIL STRATEGY #23—USE NUMBERS (BUT DON'T SPELL THEM OUT)

Numbers are powerful. Numbers grab attention.

The more numbers you use in an email for today's super-busy audience, the more you will grab their attention—and the easier it will be to "digest" your content. This includes:

- Dates
- Times
- Dollar amounts
- Statistics
- Percentages
- Numbered lists

DON'T Spell Out Numbers!

But you'll lose the power of your numbers by spelling them out. Instead, include the actual number in your content. For example:

DON'T Use These...

- One, two, three
- First, second, third
- The twenty-third of July

...Use These Instead

- 1, 2, 3
- 1st, 2nd, 3rd
- July 23

See how much faster—and easier—it is to read the second group of bullets? That's because numbers jump out of crowded text to our modern eye.

I realize that many workplaces require you to spell out numbers into words (and many style guides still recommend this). If you are required to, then do it.

But whenever you can get away with it, try using the actual numbers (without spelling them out). It's much easier to read, especially in a large block of text!

Can You Use Symbols in Email?

Absolutely! Along with using actual numbers, I routinely use the following symbols in emails—without defining them, or spelling them out in any way (unless I have a customer that specifically doesn't like when I use symbols...although that is pretty rare nowadays):

@ # $ % * + & =

Whatever you can do to make your content shorter and simpler is appreciated by most readers. Symbols are an easy way to do that!

PAULA'S EMAIL STRATEGY #24— ADD EMOJIS

Emojis are now becoming an acceptable way to express an idea or emotion in an email. Yep, even business emails.

As texting and instant messaging become more prevalent in the workplace, emojis have become more widespread in business communications also.

Emojis are a super-fast, highly efficient way to communicate a complex feeling, thought, or idea—or just to set a happy tone.

They also create a feeling of warmth, friendliness, and intimacy in written communications.

Which Emojis Are OK for Email?

To know which emojis are OK to use, think about your audience. Who will be reading this email?

Is it a business email? Or is it a more personal one—to someone you have a long-term relationship with?

The more personal the relationship, the more acceptable it is to use emojis. The most commonly used emojis that I've seen in business emails are:

Stay Away from "Negative" Emojis!

To be safe, it's better to stay away from obviously negative, offensive, or questionable emojis in the workplace. You don't want to confuse the reader by sending anything that could be considered hostile.

Even when emailing friends or long-term co-workers, I NEVER use:

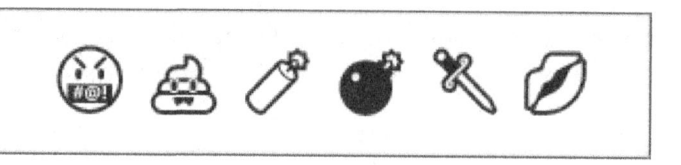

How Many Emojis Can You Use in an Email?

1-2 emojis are plenty. Don't overuse them.

If it looks like too many emojis...then it probably is!

But When in Doubt...Skip the Emojis

Emojis have become generally acceptable by most readers. But if you think your audience is too formal or conservative for emojis (or if they will judge you negatively for using them)—then don't use them.

Once you've established a good working relationship with that person, and you feel like it's more acceptable, try adding a smiley face.

It's certainly OK to wait until you've exchanged 2 or 3 messages

BEFORE you send an emoji in an email (or even to wait until they send you an emoji first!).

And sometimes, it's just better to play it safe. I don't use emojis in:

- My first email to an executive
- My first email to a client
- Any email where I'm trying to create a feeling of seriousness or formality
- Any email where I'm trying to establish expertise or credibility

Not All Email Programs Can Handle Emojis

Beware that some readers' email systems cannot translate emojis. This includes:

- Older email systems
- Some federal and government email systems
- Military email systems
- Highly secure email systems for some corporations

If their email system cannot translate your emoji, then it will come across as a weird symbol, letter, or empty box—which can backfire.

So if you're unsure whether the reader will be able to see the exact emoji you are using, then skip it.

PAULA'S EMAIL STRATEGY #25—USE A CASUAL GREETING

Boomerang did an analysis of 300,000 email messages and found that emails that use a more casual opening get a better response than emails starting with a more formal opening (like "Dear Paula" or "Greetings Paula").[28]

Best Greetings for Email

The following casual openings received the best response in the study, with up to a 64% reply rate:[29]

- Hey
- Hello
- Hi

So unless it's a situation where you feel like extra formality is absolutely required (for example, if you're emailing a 4-star general), then your best bet for a greeting is actually using the first name, along with a very casual "Hi," "Hey," or "Hello."

First Email to a Reader?

Even if it's my very first email to a person (and even if it's a C-level executive, such as a CEO or COO), I still use "Hi Angela." Just a casual, friendly "Hi"—along with their first name—is plenty.

For me, this works much better than the older, stuffier "Dear Ms. Eason."

PAULA'S EMAIL STRATEGY #26— SKIP THE FORMAL CLOSING

Just like most people today prefer a more casual greeting, they also prefer a simpler closing.

For years I closed emails with "Sincerely," "Many thanks," or "Best wishes."

However, I have not done that in at least 5 years. I started noticing a few years ago that email closings are starting to disappear.

I occasionally still see a "Thanks!" tagged onto the end of an email. But otherwise, you can now skip the formal closing altogether.

Most people today simply close their email with a signature block, and that's it. This saves a lot of time and space.

In fact, formal closings can actually work against you—since the reader may glance at it quickly and mistake your email for a form letter.

Which Emails Still Need a Formal Closing?

There are a few instances where I still add a formal closing. I usually do it when I'm emailing:

- High-ranking military leaders
- Lawyers
- Old-fashioned bosses
- Cranky neighbors and relatives
- Senior officials in the federal government

Otherwise, I just use my signature. For example:

Good Example

SUBJECT: 2:00 session in Forest Glen conf. room

Hi Sandra,

Everything is ready for the 2:00 session today. Sean Carragher will be speaking, and already has his PPT slides loaded on the laptop.

Paula Peters
Peters Writing Services, Inc.
Ph (913) 485-4537
paula@peterswriting.com
www.peterswriting.com

Notice there is no closing here—just the signature block with my name and contact info. I now close around 99% of my emails exactly like that.

PAULA'S EMAIL STRATEGY #27— BE CAREFUL WITH ATTACHMENTS

Before you send an email with an attachment, think carefully about your audience. What type of device will they use to read your email? And WHERE will they read it?

Remember the stats we cited earlier—that up to 88% of all emails are now opened on a smartphone (depending on the age of the audience).[30]

Which Device Are They Using to Read Your Email?

If your reader uses a desktop or laptop...
If your reader is opening your email on a desktop or laptop, then the attachment is easy to read—so you have a pretty good chance that he or she will open it.

However, keep in mind that as few as 9.8% of all emails are now opened on a desktop.[31]

Also, even if the reader IS reading your email on a desktop, chances are that they still have a pretty short attention span. In other words, they may be too busy, too impatient, or too unwilling to read an attachment.

In that case, try using one of the suggestions below.

If Your Reader Uses a Smartphone...

If your reader opens their email on a smartphone, it gets a little trickier to send attachments. Think about this:

- Do they have the right app to open the attachment?
- Is the smartphone display big enough?
- Will the font be too small?
- Will the document download correctly over a cellular connection?
- Is the document too long to read by phone? (Very few people read an attachment longer than 1-2 p. on a smartphone.)

If you KNOW your reader will use a smartphone (and you have the ability to post the document to a website), try using a hyperlink instead. I find that people are happy to open a hyperlink, rather than an attachment.

What if You Don't Know Which Device They're Using to Read Your Email?

It's best to assume they're using a smartphone. Why? Because you don't want to risk the possibility of someone missing the attachment altogether.

Ideas for Reviewing Attachments by Email

Here are a few alternate strategies I've used successfully, instead of sending an attachment:

- **If it's a short document (1-2 p. max)**—try using a quick 1-2 sentence introduction, then copy and paste the entire body content of the document directly into the email. This is easier for most people than downloading/opening an attachment.
- **Tell them upfront how long it will take to read the document**—if you say, for example, "This should take less than 1 minute to read," you'll get more people to read it.
- **Give them a darn good reason WHY they should open the attachment**—by saying something like, "You may lose your health benefits if you don't review the attachment," you'll probably get more people to read the attachment.
- **Use a hyperlink**—try posting the document to a website, then add a hyperlink to that document in your email. I find that people will click a link before they'll open an attachment, especially on a smartphone. (Even better—create a bit.ly for a shorter hyperlink.)

Try Combining Multiple Strategies Together

You can also use several of these strategies together. For example, you can add the attachment AND a hyperlink—AND paste the content into the body of the email—AND give a good reason why it's important, AND tell them exactly how long it will take to read.

Combining multiple strategies together gives you a better chance of the user actually reading your content!

PAULA'S EMAIL STRATEGY #28—ADD AN EXCLAMATION POINT!

For many years, my English teachers taught me that exclamation points are taboo in official documents. And in the 1990s and early 2000s, this was definitely true.

However, in recent years, as technology has transformed email to be more casual—the exclamation point has returned.

Today, using an exclamation point in an email is perfectly acceptable.

It shows you are friendly, approachable, and a "real human." In other words, the email is not just a form letter.

It even establishes a warm connection in an email. Let me show you an example of how this works.

How Many Exclamation Points Can You Use?

I recommend sticking to only 1 (or maybe 2) exclamation points in a single email:

Good Example

SUBJECT: 2nd quarter profit

Hi Bethany,

Did you see that we posted a 4.2% profit for the 2nd quarter? Nice work!

I look forward to seeing you next week!

Paula

Bad Example

SUBJECT: 2nd quarter profit

Hi Bethany,

We posted a 4.2% profit for the 2nd quarter. Nice work.

I look forward to seeing you next week.

Paula

See the difference? The first email sounds a lot more "friendly," and creates a warm connection with the reader by using 2 exclamation points.

The second email, without the exclamation points, seems more formal.

What if a Reader Is More Conservative?

If you're concerned that the reader is too conservative (or old-school) for an exclamation point, then skip it.

But it definitely adds a "human touch" to an otherwise dry, business-focused email.

PAULA'S EMAIL STRATEGY #29— SEND THE EMAIL TO YOURSELF FIRST

Here's a really easy hack that professional writers use all the time. Before I click "send" on an email to an important reader, I send the email to myself first.

Specifically, I send the email to my SMARTPHONE first.

This lets me see EXACTLY how it's going to look when it's received by the customer, CEO, or 2-star general. Because most likely, they'll be reading my email on a smartphone.

And since I'm usually typing my emails on a laptop or desktop, I don't know EXACTLY how they're going to look when they appear in a smartphone app.

Sometimes, I even send it to a few different email apps (or devices) to see how it looks. For example, I might send a test email to:

- My personal Gmail—on iPad
- MS Outlook—on my laptop
- Hotmail—on my Android phone
- Internet email app—on my desktop

Try a Test Email...First

When I open my test email in different email apps, here's what I look for:

- Can I see the entire subject line?
- Are the paragraph "chunks" too big?
- Are the sentences too long?
- Is the font too small?
- Does the body font look right?
- Are emojis showing up correctly?
- Is there any other way I can make it look better on the tiny smartphone screen?
- Do I have to scroll down to read the entire email? (very few people scroll down)

Once I see it, I usually go back into the email and make a few final tweaks to these before sending the final draft:

- Fonts
- Content length
- Paragraph chunks
- Sentence length
- Overall layout
- Subheaders
- Images
- Subject line

You don't have to do this for every email...but it really helps an important email stand out from the crowd!

PAULA'S EMAIL STRATEGY #30— CHANGE THE SUBJECT LINE ON REPLIES AND FORWARDS

Occasionally, an email string has so many replies and forwards from different people that the original conversation no longer connects to the subject line.

So...can you change the subject line? Of course!

I always change my subject line to match the current topic or question. Readers appreciate it

Summarizing a Complex Message String

It can get very difficult to scan through multiple email messages to understand the key points.

If you're adding to a long, complex message string that you're forwarding (or replying to), don't say "see below" to reference a question or fact. Most readers are too busy to do this.

Instead, write a brief, 1-sentence recap of what they need to know in bold letters in your current message.

PAULA'S EMAIL STRATEGY #31—STOP THE CYA MADNESS

Sending a CYA ("cover your ass") email was popular in the corporate world in the 1990s and early 2000s. By sending a cc: email to your boss, you made sure they knew what was happening:

- On your project
- In your department
- On your team
- On a difficult issue with a customer
- In a conflict with a team member, or another department

However, so many leaders receive 300, 400, or 500 emails every day that the CYA email has become a hassle.

Managers Are Too Busy to Read CYA Emails Today

When I ask senior leaders about their email habits, most tell me that they simply do not read any emails they are copied (cc'd) on. This goes for corporate executives, high-ranking government officials, and senior military officers alike.

In fact, as a survival strategy, most executives that I interview say they automatically file, hide, or delete these emails from their inbox, so they can focus instead on answering emails where they are listed on the "To:" line. (Unless the email comes from their boss—or from the CEO, for example).

Ask Your Boss!

Be respectful of your boss's time. If you're unsure about whether to cc: your boss on your emails, then ask them for their preferences.

If you copy them on lots of emails, try asking them directly if they want you to continue doing that:

> "Hey Sheila, I've been copying you on a lot of emails lately. I don't want to overload your inbox. Should I keep copying you on all these emails? Or do you want me to stop?"

I occasionally meet a manager in my classes who likes to read their CYA emails, although it seems like there are fewer and fewer of them every year.

Another option: simply stop copying your boss on your emails and see what happens. If they don't say anything, then they probably weren't reading them anyway.

You can always start again if they say, "Hey! How come I haven't seen your emails lately?"

BONUS STRATEGY #1 —NEW EMAIL TRENDS

As emails get shorter and shorter, I've noticed a few new trends. You may have noticed these, too.

Occasionally, I meet people that are offended by these trends—but there's no reason to be.

They're simply new ways to make email communication more speedy and efficient.

Empty Emails ("Subject Line Only")

More and more, I see emails that mimic texts and instant messages. One example of this is what I call an "empty email."

Have you seen this yet?

SUBJECT: I'll be at your desk at noon for lunch

Paula Peters
Peters Writing Services, Inc.
Ph (913) 485-4537
paula@peterswriting.com
www.peterswriting.com

There's usually a long subject line, including an action or a question—but ZERO body content.

Basically, it's a text message sent through email. These are becoming more and more common, and also more acceptable—especially with intra-office email.

These are fine to use and save the reader a lot of time. But I only recommend using them with a co-worker or friend, where you have a long-term established email relationship.

No Greeting

As emails evolve to look more like texts, I've also noticed that greetings are getting shorter—and sometimes disappearing entirely.

Every year, I receive more and more emails without a greeting. The writer just gets straight to the action.

It usually looks like this:

> **SUBJECT: Lunch today?**
>
> I'll swing by your desk at noon—if you still want to go to Red Robin.
>
> Paula Peters
> **Peters Writing Services, Inc.**
> Ph (913) 485-4537
> paula@peterswriting.com
> www.peterswriting.com

There's no reason to be offended by the casualness (or lack of greeting) here. This is simply a faster, more efficient way of emailing the people we communicate with on a daily basis.

Don't Try This with New Contacts!

I recommend saving this email technique for someone you know really well or have worked with for a long time.

It's a great time-saver for long-term, established working relationships—but can actually be offensive if used with someone you don't know very well.

I personally would NOT use this technique with:

- New contacts
- New clients
- New co-workers
- Your boss
- An executive

BONUS STRATEGY #2—EMAILING A CONSERVATIVE AUDIENCE

Yes, there are still a few readers out there who are more conservative in email.

In my experience, I have found many (but not all) of the following to be more formal in their emails:

- Bankers
- Lawyers
- Professors/academics
- Surgeons (and other medical personnel)
- Scientists/researchers
- Senior military leaders
- (Some) old-school business executives
- (Some) legislators/government staff

Knowing if the Audience Is More Conservative

Sometimes, it's hard to tell if you're dealing with a conservative audience—especially on the very first message.

If you receive emails from the person that are dry, formal,

long-winded, and stiff (with l-o-n-g paragraphs and l-o-n-g sentences), then your best bet is to respond in the same format.

Match the conservative tone of the person who emailed you. For example, let's say you receive an email that looks like this:

SUBJECT: Holiday luncheon

Dear Mrs. Zygmunt,

We request your presence at the annual holiday luncheon on December 23rd. Service begins at 11:30 am. Formal business attire is required.

Please RSVP your attendance to x4745 with your delights or regrets as quickly as possible.

Respectfully yours,

Franklin B. Preston

This email is pretty formal, so it's better to stay on the safe side. Send a formal reply. In this case, a good reply might be:

Good Example

SUBJECT: Holiday luncheon

Dear Mr. Preston,

Thank you for the personal invitation to the holiday luncheon on December 23rd. I have replied "yes" to x4745, and I look forward to seeing you at 11:30 am on the day of the event.

Best wishes,

Paula

When in doubt, you can always "play it safe" by matching the tone, length, and style of the sender's email.

What if This Is Your First Email to Someone?

If this is your first email to a boss, co-worker, client, or executive, then it's totally OK to be more formal with the tone and style of your email.

Play it safe by starting off with a more conservative tone in the first email, then wait to see their reply.

If their reply email is more casual, then your second email can be more casual.

But if they reply in a very stiff, formal manner, then it's better to follow their lead—and continue to be formal in your own emails.

Once You've Developed a Relationship...

Once you've developed a friendly working relationship with your boss, co-worker, client, or executive, then you can feel more comfortable getting casual. Try using some of the tricks and techniques in this book.

What if Their Emails Are ALWAYS Formal?

In some cases, you may have a boss, co-worker, professor, or client that simply prefers formal emails—no matter how long you've worked with them.

If they are consistently stiff and formal in their emails, then you'll probably get a better response if you match their conservative tone and style.

Just don't get TOO long-winded! Everyone is moving faster today—whether they are conservative or not.

12 EXAMPLES OF BAD EMAILS—DON'T STEAL THESE!

Here are 12 examples of BAD emails that I've collected over the years. You definitely DON'T want to follow these examples![‡]

Each one makes a critical mistake, such as being:

- Long
- Complicated
- Vague
- Wordy
- Dense
- Unclear
- Impolite

Some of these email examples are taken from the chapters in this book (I've edited several to stand alone, just in case you headed directly to this chapter). I've also added a few new ones here.

#Fail!—Complicated Reply Required

SUBJECT: Help??

Hi Allison,

The new copier is broken—and the Nelson trial starts on

Monday. What should we do?? Help!!

Paula

#Fail!—Unnecessary Urgency

SUBJECT: URGENT—need lunch for meeting

Hi Jules,

URGENT—we need the lunch order submitted NOW. Our meeting starts with the client @ 1:00 pm in the Sky Room. The cutoff time is 3-4 hrs. BEFORE.

Thanks!

Paula

#Fail!—Not Explaining "Why"

SUBJECT: Healthcare benefits

Dear David,

Click the link below to register for healthcare benefits. The deadline is midnight on Dec. 1st.

Thank you!

Paula

#Fail!—Not Requesting Action

SUBJECT: Expense reports

Hi Nico,

Here are the 3 expense reports from the Dallas trip. Employees would like to receive their checks before mandatory shutdown. So it would be great if they could be approved by COB on Friday.

Thanks!

Paula

#Fail!—High Reading Level

SUBJECT: Request for training proposal

Good afternoon, Ms. Peters!

We are populating our first quarter of the fiscal year, and your technical writing courses are vital to our continued success. We would like to host you in September for three days of your technical writing training, titled "7 Professional Writing Secrets—to Write Better, Faster, Easier," and structured as such:

- Day 1 – 8-hour course
- Day 2 – 8-hour course (for a targeted group)
- Day 3 – 1-hour course (designated for strategic executives)

We are continuing with selection for other quarters in the upcoming fiscal year, but right now, we want to inquire into your availability to conduct this course (ideally in September). We'd like to engage in the near future for additional sessions throughout the year.

As you know from past collaborations, scheduling can often be our first hurdle. Given the level of these training events, we have several considerations on our end and realize that you have a very busy schedule as well.

We appreciate you working with us and look forward to continuing our relationship with you!

Very respectfully,

Michael

#Fail!—Too Many Pleasantries

SUBJECT: Estimate for client project

Dear Karla,

It was great seeing you at lunch yesterday. I really enjoyed talking about the project with you. I think we are going to align well on finishing this up together, and I'm excited about bringing this to the finish line.

By the way—could you please review the attached project scope, and send me an estimate by 3:00 pm tomorrow? Thanks!

Paula

#Fail!—Needs Subheaders

SUBJECT: Holiday party planning meeting

Hi Emily,

Thank you for helping us plan the holiday party! We're all going to meet at 9:30 am on Monday, November 10th in the Ellis Room on the 7th floor. Jessica, Susan, Scott, and Zack will be there too.

I'll be asking you about the projector and screen rental, plus the PowerPoint slides with photos that you talked about running—so be sure to bring information on those. Look forward to seeing you there!

Paula

#Fail!—Needs Bullets

SUBJECT: Invoice review

Hi Joe,

When you get a minute, we'll need you to please review the attached: prepayment invoice, proposal agreement, and certificate of insurance. Just sign and return when you are done. Thanks!

Paula

#Fail!—Too Many Questions

SUBJECT: Pick up office supplies?

Hi Taylor,

Could you swing by and pick up some office supplies on the way to XYZ Company's office? We're out of black ink.

Oh, and by the way—did you have time to put together the agenda for the Tues. meeting? Remember that Aiden will be attending this week. Did you include his action items?

Thanks!

Paula

#Fail!—Old-Fashioned Narrative Voice

SUBJECT: Cardholder's overdue account

Dear cardholder,

It has come to the attention of this company that the above account is past due. Account holder should please advise in writing on when this issue will be resolved, and whether the bank can provide any assistance in this matter.

Respectfully,

Ms. Paula Peters

#Fail!—Too Negative

SUBJECT: The Marsten account is messed up

Hi Tony,

I'm still waiting for you to give me an update about the Marsten account. I've already sent you 3 emails about this.

Could you get off your butt and do something about this? Please?? We're going to be late on our deadline!

Thanks,

Paula

#Fail!—Shouting

SUBJECT: Budget worksheet

Hi Steve,

I need an electronic copy of the budget worksheet AS SOON AS POSSIBLE. DO YOU UNDERSTAND? This absolutely NEEDS TO BE COMPLETED by OCTOBER 29TH.

Paula

50 EXAMPLES OF GOOD EMAILS— PLEASE STEAL THESE!

Now let's look at 50 examples of GOOD emails that utilize the tricks, hacks, and techniques from this book.

I encourage you to steal, borrow, edit, or recycle ANY of this content for your own emails![s]

I have included many GOOD examples from the book's content (some are edited to work better as stand-alone examples), plus added a bunch of new ones too.

Can you see the difference between these GOOD examples—and the BAD examples I shared in the previous chapter?

Meeting Invitation Email

SUBJECT: Discuss the client presentation?

Hi Lynda,

Would you be interested in getting together—to talk about our upcoming client presentation with Glaxo?

I'd love to get your input on how you think we should approach them. If you're interested, how about Thursday at 3:30 pm—at the Panera next door?

Paula

Reschedule Meeting Email

SUBJECT: Reschedule lunch?

Hi Fred,

Would you like to try meeting again this Fri. at 11:30 am—at that little Italian bistro on 39th St.?

Let me know if that works for you. Hope to see you then!

Paula

Cancel Meeting Email

SUBJECT: Cancel our meeting?

Hi Kay,

Would you mind if we canceled our Tuesday meeting? I have a conflict with a family appointment.

If it's OK with you, maybe we could move it to Thursday @ 11:30 am? Thanks!

Paula

Request Urgent Action Email—#1

SUBJECT: Submit lunch order by 9:30 am?

Hi Jules,

Could you submit the lunch order by 9:30 am? Our meeting starts with the client in the Sky Room @ 1:00 pm—and the catering service needs a 3-4 hr. heads-up.

Thanks for your help!

Paula

Request Urgent Action Email—#2

SUBJECT: Your healthcare benefits expire next week

Hi David,

You could lose your healthcare benefits for next year if you don't complete your registration by midnight on Dec. 1st.

Could you please click the link below to register? Thank you so much!

Paula

SUBJECT: Approve expense reports by COB Friday?

Hi Nico,

Could you please approve the 3 attached expense reports from the Dallas trip by COB on Friday? Then employees will receive their checks before mandatory shutdown.

Thanks!

Paula

Request Proposal Email

SUBJECT: Software proposal—from your team?

Hi Janelle,

We'd love to learn more about your point-of-sale software, including the price—and how it works. Could you send us a proposal by April 30th?

Let me know if that date works for you. Thanks…we look forward to hearing from you!

Paula

Accept A Proposal Email

SUBJECT: Your software proposal

Hi Janelle,

We really liked your proposal for the point-of-sale software—and we'd like to get started right away. What's the next step in your process?

Thank you so much for your help. We're excited to work with you!

Paula

Reject A Proposal Email

SUBJECT: Your software proposal

Hi Janelle,

We loved your proposal for the point-of-sale software—but unfortunately, the pricing was too expensive for our budget.

We really appreciate you taking the time to come to our office and give us a demonstration, and we'd be happy to pass along your name to other folks as a referral. Thank you!

Paula

Renegotiate A Proposal Email

SUBJECT: Your software proposal

Hi Janelle,

We loved your proposal for the point-of-sale software, and I think it could benefit our customers—but we felt like it was out of our budget.

Would you consider lowering the annual subscription price by just $250? If so, we'd love to sign an agreement with you for 10 licenses.

Thank you!

Paula

Short Proposal Email

SUBJECT: Price for your article

Hi Anthony,

Sure, I'd be happy to write the article for you on conveyor belts. If this estimate works, just email me a written approval and I'll get started:

- **500-word article**—interview contacts, research technical specs, write 1 draft, do 2 rounds of revisions, perform graphic layout, final proofread = $350

Thanks!

Paula

Positive Feedback Email

SUBJECT: Completion of the Zigzag project

Hi Molly,

You did an excellent job completing the Zigzag project 9 days early—and meeting all of your deliverables. I appreciate your attention to detail, your ability to manage multiple deadlines, and your flexibility working with all the people involved.

Thank you so much for your awesome contribution to our team!

Paula

Negative Feedback Email

SUBJECT: Completion of the Zigzag project

Hi Molly,

Thank you so much for all the hard work you put into the Zigzag project. You did a tremendous job of coordinating multiple deadlines and working with all the different people involved. I really appreciate your attention to detail!

Unfortunately, the client wasn't excited about the final result, and the fact that we came in 3 days late. Is there anything we can do differently next time—to make sure we get the project done on time? Or maybe set their expectations upfront—about final deliverables and timeline?

Thank you so much for your work. I look forward to hearing your thoughts!

Paula

Request Feedback Email

SUBJECT: What do you think—final blueprint?

Hi Shahid,

We just posted the final draft of the room layout to our Intranet folder, C://MeetingSpace. What do you think of the spacing and flow? Will this work better for you?

I'd love to hear your thoughts. Looking forward to getting your feedback!

Paula

Schedule Event Email

SUBJECT: Can you provide training in September?

Hi Paula,

We're scheduling a few classes for next year...and we'd love for you to teach your popular writing class, "7 Professional Writing Secrets—to Write Better, Faster, Easier," in September!

Do you have any dates available for the following?

- Day 1 – 8-hour course
- Day 2 – 8-hour course (for one single group)
- Day 3 – 1-hour course (a few specific executives)

We're still looking at other dates to bring you back for the rest of the year—but first just want to see if you're free in September.

We're pretty busy—and we know you are too!—so the sooner we can get it on the calendar, the better.

You are awesome to work with, and we're excited to see you here again. Thank you so much!

Michael

Event Reminder Email

SUBJECT: Birthday today in breakroom

Hey Marty,

Don't forget—there's cake in the breakroom today at 1:15 pm for Julie's birthday. See you then! #NeedABreak #Yum #LoveThisJob #NeverEnoughCake

Paula

Multiple Choice Email

SUBJECT: Broken copier?

Hi Allison,

The new copy machine is broken—and we're unable to complete the copies for the Nelson trial. What would you like me to do?

    A. Call a repairman from ProCopy Systems
    B. Borrow a copier from the 3rd floor—just to prep for trial
    C. Order a new copier to be delivered—from Office-Max

Paula

Recommend Solution Email

SUBJECT: Can I call a repair man?

Hi Allison,

The new copy machine is broken—and the Nelson trial starts Monday. Could I:

- Call a repairman from ProCopy Systems? (should be under $100)

Let me know if that works for you. Thanks!

Paula

Pitch Idea Email

SUBJECT: Could we try this?

Hi Wesley,

We're still not reaching our committed target of 350+ calls/month. Would it be OK if we tried this?

- Ask all entry-level interns to research 2 call leads daily and log them in Salesforce.com—before calls begin at 9:00 am

That would reduce the amount of time wasted by our sales staff by approx. 8 min./call.

Let me know if that works for you. Thanks!

Paula

Request A Document Email

SUBJECT: Final report—for Marsten account?

Hi Tony,

I've really enjoyed working with you over the past 6 months on the Marsten account. Would you mind emailing me the final report in Excel—by May 17?

That way, we can still meet our deadline without involving our VP. Thank you so much for your awesome work on this project!

Paula

SUBJECT: Budget worksheet

Hi LaTonya,

Could you please send me an electronic copy of the budget worksheet—as soon as you have a moment? We're submitting the final proposal to the Dept. of Defense on Wed.

Thanks!

Paula

Review A Document Email

SUBJECT: Estimate for client project

Hi Karla,

Could you please review this project scope for our client, and send me an estimate by 3:00 pm tomorrow?

By the way...it was great seeing you at lunch yesterday!

Paula

Proofread A Document Email

SUBJECT: Could you proof this letter?

Hi Heidi,

Would you mind proofing the final draft of the 1 p. offer letter to the new Sales Manager—before I send it? I want to make sure there's no mistakes.

Let me know if you have time. That would be awesome. Thank you!
Paula

Due Date Email

SUBJECT: Your entry form?

Hi Scott,

Just a reminder—your **entry form** must be received **by June 25th** in order to qualify for the awards program.

Thank you!

Paula

Provide Instructions Email

SUBJECT: Your entry form?

Hi Scott,

Just a reminder—your entry form must be received **by June 25th** in order to qualify for the awards program. There are multiple categories you can submit to. Please choose your **best 3 categories on your entry form**.

In addition, you will be required to submit an attachment for each of your top 3 categories. Be sure to **submit 1 work sample for each category** on your entry form (for a **total of 3 work samples**).

Thank you!
Paula

Request Help Email

SUBJECT: Potluck setup?

Hi Avery and Jessamyn,

Is there any chance you could help us set up the training room for the potluck lunch today? **Jessamyn**—we could use your awesome decorating skills! **Avery**—we'd love to borrow the extra table from your office.

Thanks so much!
Paula

Delegate A Task Email

SUBJECT: Completing the project matrix

Hi Roger,

By any chance, would you have time to assist Jim with completing the project matrix for our customer call data in Excel—before Thursday? (Please incl. columns for client name, date, issue, and status.)

That would help us ALL meet the COO's deadline for Friday. Let me know if you'd be available to help with this. Thank you in advance!

Paula

Decline A Task Email

SUBJECT: Your PowerPoint presentation...

Hi Bill,

I'd love to help you put together the slides for your PowerPoint presentation, but I'm booked in meetings all day Tuesday and Wednesday.

Is there someone else who might be able to assist you? I'm so sorry to leave you hanging!

Paula

Coordinate Meeting Email

SUBJECT: Holiday party planning meeting

Hi Jacob,

Thank you for helping us plan the holiday party!

DATE/TIME
Monday, November 10th—9:30 am

LOCATION

Ellis Room—7th floor

ATTENDEES
- Jessica
- Susan
- Scott
- Zack
- Jacob
- Paula

ACTION ITEMS
- **Jacob**—projector/screen rental + PowerPoint slides with photos
- **Susan**—food from caterer
- **Zack**—lighting and electrical requirements
- **Jessica**—napkins, plates, forks, serving dishes, etc.

Look forward to seeing you there!

Paula

Coordinate Lunch Email

SUBJECT: Lunch next week?

Hi Morgan,

I could meet for lunch next week—Tues., Wed., or Fri. Would any of those days work for you?

Looking forward to it!

Paula

Use Bullets In Email

SUBJECT: Can you review this?

Hi Joe,

Could you please review the attached docs when you get a minute?

- Prepayment invoice
- Proposal agreement
- Certificate of insurance

Just sign each item, scan, and return by email when you're done. Thanks!

Paula

Payment Request Email

SUBJECT: Here's your invoice—please pay by May 31st

Hi Susan,

Here's your invoice (attached). If you'd prefer to pay by credit card, just let me know—and I can send you an email payment link.

We accept any type of credit or debit card. Thanks!

Paula

Overdue Payment Email—#1

SUBJECT: Did you receive our invoice?

Hi Susan,

Could you please check and see if you received our invoice for $324.00 on May 31? I haven't received a check yet, and I wanted to make sure it didn't get lost in the mail.

And if you'd rather pay by credit card, just let me know—I'll send you an email link. Thanks!

Paula

Overdue Payment Email—#2

SUBJECT: Did you send payment?

Hi Susan,

I still haven't received payment for our 5/31 invoice for $324. Right now, it's 45 days overdue.

Can you let me know the check #, and when you mailed it?

Just a heads-up—if we don't receive payment by 7/31, then our tech support team usually deactivates the software link.

Also, if you'd rather pay by credit card, I can send you an email link. Thanks!

Paula

Ask For A Favor Email

SUBJECT: Pick up office supplies?

Hi Taylor,

Could you pick up some office supplies today—on the way to XYZ Company's office? We're out of black ink.

If you have time, that would be awesome. :) Thanks!

Paula

Multiple Actions Request Email

SUBJECT: Corp taxes due next week

Hi Colin and Alexa,

Corporate taxes are due next week. **Colin**—can you send

me all the employee receipts by Thursday? And **Alexa**—can you send me the final expense list for Q1-Q4? Thanks!

Paula

SUBJECT: Corp taxes due next week

Hi Colin, Alexa, Tristan,

Corporate taxes are due next week. Can you help me with the following items?

- **Colin**—can you send all employee receipts by Thursday?
- **Alexa**—can you send final expense list for Q1-Q4?
- **Tristan**—can you forward copies of all completed audit forms to Ryan by tomorrow?

Thank you SO much!

Paula

Confirmation Email

SUBJECT: Going to meeting?

Hi Debbie,

Are you planning to attend the year-end mtg. on Tues. @ 3:00 pm? It should only be 30 min. long.

Let me know if you can't make it for any reason. Thank you!

Paula

Accept Invitation Email

SUBJECT: Holiday party on Dec. 17th

Hi Nancy,

Thank you so much for inviting me to the holiday party. I'll be there!

Paula

Decline Invitation Email

SUBJECT: Holiday party on Dec. 17th

Hi Nancy,

I'm so sorry I won't be able to make the holiday party on Dec. 17th. Thank you so much for inviting me—hopefully, I can attend next year!

Paula

Formal Invitation Reply Email

SUBJECT: Holiday luncheon

Dear Mr. Preston,

Thank you for the personal invitation to the holiday luncheon scheduled for December 23rd. I have replied "yes" to x4745, and I look forward to seeing you at 11:30 am on that day.

Best wishes,

Paula

Accept New Employee Email

SUBJECT: Job opportunity—St. Mary's Hospital

Hi Martin,

Thank you so much for coming to our office last week. We'd love to offer you the position of Senior Sales Director.

Our human resources executive, Rosa Wilson, will contact

you within the next 1-2 weeks to begin the new employee registration process. Welcome aboard!

Paula

Decline Employee Candidate Email

SUBJECT: Job opportunity—St. Mary's Hospital

Hi Martin,

Thank you so much for coming to our office last week. We really enjoyed talking to you.

We have decided to offer the position of Senior Sales Director to a different candidate. However, we really liked your experience and resume.

Would it be OK if we kept your information in our files—to consider for other positions?

Thank you again for sharing your time with us!

Paula

Request Job Info Email

SUBJECT: Technical writer—Advent Pharmaceuticals?

Hi Louann,

I noticed that your company is currently looking for a full-time technical writer for your St. Louis office. I've written more than 450+ healthcare white papers, articles, instruction manuals, and web pages at SupraCare Health over the past 3 years.

Could I send you my resume for consideration? Thanks! I'm at 913-485-4537, or paula@peterswriting.com.

Paula

Request Job Interview Email

SUBJECT: Job opportunity—Advent Pharmaceuticals?

Hi Louann,

I noticed that you have a position open for a full-time technical writer. I've written more than 450+ healthcare white papers, articles, instruction manuals, and web pages for SupraCare Health over the past 3 years.

Would you be interested in meeting for 10 min. by phone—to see if I might be a good fit for your organization? I'm at 913-485-4537, or paula@peterswriting.com.

Thanks!

Paula

Recruiter Cover Letter Email

SUBJECT: Tech writer opportunity—Advent Pharmaceuticals

Hi Louann,

I was very excited to learn about your full-time tech writer position at the St. Louis office.

I've written more than 450+ healthcare white papers, articles, instruction manuals, and web pages for SupraCare Health over the past 3 years, and I'd love to help your team.

If you have time, I'd be happy to meet with you to see if it's a good fit. I'm at 913-485-4537, or paula@peterswriting.com.

My resume is attached. Thanks for considering!

Paula

Job Interview Follow-Up Email

SUBJECT: Job opportunity—Advent Pharmaceuticals?

Hi Louann,

I really enjoyed meeting with you last week. Thank you for taking the time to interview me!

I'm wondering if your team has made a decision yet about the job? I'd love to work with Advent, and I look forward to hearing from you.

Thank you!

Paula

Recruiter Thank You Email

SUBJECT: Thank you for the opportunity!

Hi Louann,

Thanks for your email. I totally understand that I'm not a good fit for the position right now, and I appreciate you meeting with me last week to learn about my experience.

Thank you so much for your time!

Paula

Basic Thank You Email

SUBJECT: Thanks for the Q2 report!

Hi Jordan,

Thank you so much for getting the Q2 report to me early. This will help me get the final statements to the CFO before Monday. I really appreciate it!

Paula

"Nice Job" Email

SUBJECT: 2nd quarter profit

Hi Bethany,

Did you see that we posted a 4.2% profit for the 2nd quarter? You and your team did an excellent job of meeting a tight deadline—to make this happen.

Thank you so much for your effort. Nice work!

Paula

SOURCES

Acton, Annabel. "How to Stop Wasting 2.5 Hours on Email Every Day." *Forbes*. July 13, 2017. https://www.forbes.com/sites/annabelacton/2017/07/13/innovators-challenge-how-to-stop-wasting-time-on-emails/#54da4c309788

Bhujwala, Amreen. "6 Ways to Use Personalization in Email Subject Lines for Better Open Rates." *Constant Contact*. January 2020. https://blogs.constantcontact.com/personalization-in-email-subject-lines/

G., Brendan. "How to Start an Email: An Email Openings Analysis of 300,000+ Messages." *Boomerang*. December 14, 2017. https://blog.boomerangapp.com/2017/12/how-to-start-an-email-an-email-openings-analysis/

Moore, Alex. "7 Tips for Getting More Responses to Your Emails (With Data!). *Boomerang*. February 12, 2016. http://blog.boomerangapp.com/2016/02/7-tips-for-getting-more-responses-to-your-emails-with-data/

Naragon, Kristin. "Subject: Email, We Just Can't Get Enough." *Adobe Blog*. August 26, 2015. https://theblog.adobe.com/email/

Pierce, David, and Lauren Goode. "The WIRED Guide to the iPhone." *WIRED*. December 7, 2018. https://www.wired.com/story/guide-iphone/

Ryan, Camille L. and Kurt Bauman. "Educational Attainment in the United States: 2015." *U.S. Census Bureau*. March 2016. https://www.census.gov/content/dam/Census/library/publications/2016/demo/p20-578.pdf

Stillman, Jessica. "The Perfect Length for an Email Subject Line." *Inc.* June 20, 2014. https://www.inc.com/jessica-stillman/the-perfect-length-for-an-email-subject-line.html

Upland Adestra. "Top 10 Email Clients in March 2019." January 2020. https://uplandsoftware.com/adestra/resources/blog/top-10-email-clients/

White, Chad. "Email Attention Spans Are Growing." *Salesforce.com.* March 28, 2017. https://www.salesforce.com/blog/2017/03/email-attention-spans-are-growing.html

NOTES

[*] Interestingly, that stat has increased significantly from about 8 seconds...4 years ago. Most likely, it's because people are being more selective about which emails to read and deleting more emails in general.

[†] Interesting side note—I'm starting to see a few K-12 schools and colleges shift their focus to the newer, shorter style of writing presented in this book. For example, my daughter is in 4th grade at a public school in Kansas. She presents most of her reports in PowerPoint, or video (using tools like ChatterPix), which favors shorter, simpler sentences. My son (in 8th grade) has had a similar experience—more visual presentations of data and learning than ever before. But then other schools nearby don't seem to be doing that at all, and are still using the older format of delivering reports—long documents in Microsoft Word.

[‡] However, keep in mind that if your boss, client, or executive wants you to write like this...then please do it!

[§] Just don't forget to change the names!

[1] Chad White. "Email Attention Spans Are Growing." Salesforce.com. March 28, 2017. https://www.salesforce.com/blog/2017/03/email-attention-spans-are-growing.html

[2] Annabel Acton. "How to Stop Wasting 2.5 Hours on Email Every Day." Forbes. July 13, 2017. https://www.forbes.com/sites/annabelacton/2017/07/13/innovators-challenge-how-to-stop-wasting-time-on-emails/#54da4c309788

[3] Annabel Acton. "How to Stop Wasting 2.5 Hours on Email Every Day." Forbes. July 13, 2017. https://www.forbes.com/sites/annabelacton/2017/07/13/innovators-challenge-how-to-stop-wasting-time-on-emails/#54da4c309788

[4] Upland Adestra. "Top 10 Email Clients in March 2019." 2020. https://uplandsoftware.com/adestra/resources/blog/top-10-email-clients/

[5] Kristin Naragon. "Subject: Email, We Just Can't Get Enough." Adobe Blog. August 26, 2015. https://theblog.adobe.com/email/

[6] Annabel Acton. "How to Stop Wasting 2.5 Hours on Email Every Day." Forbes. July 13, 2017. https://www.forbes.com/sites/annabelacton/2017/07/13/innovators-challenge-how-to-stop-wasting-time-on-emails/#54da4c309788

[7] Kristin Naragon. "Subject: Email, We Just Can't Get Enough." Adobe Blog. August 26, 2015. https://theblog.adobe.com/email/

[8] Upland Adestra. "Top 10 Email Clients in March 2019." 2020. https://uplandsoftware.com/adestra/resources/blog/top-10-email-clients/

[9] Annabel Acton. "How to Stop Wasting 2.5 Hours on Email Every Day." Forbes. July 13, 2017. https://www.forbes.com/sites/annabelacton/2017/07/13/innovators-challenge-how-to-stop-wasting-time-on-emails/#54da4c309788

[10] Upland Adestra. "Top 10 Email Clients in March 2019." January 2020. https://uplandsoftware.com/adestra/resources/blog/top-10-email-clients/

[11] Kristin Naragon. "Subject: Email, We Just Can't Get Enough." Adobe Blog. August 26, 2015. https://theblog.adobe.com/email/

[12] David Pierce and Lauren Goode. "The WIRED Guide to the iPhone." WIRED. December 7, 2018. https://www.wired.com/story/guide-iphone/

[13] David Pierce and Lauren Goode. "The WIRED Guide to the iPhone." WIRED. December 7, 2018. https://www.wired.com/story/guide-iphone/

[14] Jessica Stillman. "The Perfect Length for an Email Subject Line." Inc. June 20, 2014. https://www.inc.com/jessica-stillman/the-perfect-length-for-an-email-subject-line.html

[15] Alex Moore. "7 Tips for Getting More Responses to Your Emails (With Data!). *Boomerang.* February 12, 2016. http://blog.boomerangapp.com/2016/02/7-tips-for-getting-more-responses-to-your-emails-with-data/

[16] Annabel Acton. "How to Stop Wasting 2.5 Hours on Email Every Day." Forbes. July 13, 2017. https://www.forbes.com/sites/annabelacton/2017/07/13/innovators-challenge-how-to-stop-wasting-time-on-emails/#54da4c309788

[17] Alex Moore. "7 Tips for Getting More Responses to Your Emails (With Data!). *Boomerang.* February 12, 2016. http://blog.boomerangapp.com/2016/02/7-tips-for-getting-more-responses-to-your-emails-with-data/

[18] Alex Moore. "7 Tips for Getting More Responses to Your Emails (With Data!). *Boomerang.* February 12, 2016. http://blog.boomerangapp.com/2016/02/7-tips-for-getting-more-responses-to-your-emails-with-data/

[19] Upland Adestra. "Top 10 Email Clients in March 2019." 2020. https://uplandsoftware.com/adestra/resources/blog/top-10-email-clients/

[20] Kristin Naragon. "Subject: Email, We Just Can't Get Enough." Adobe Blog.

August 26, 2015. https://theblog.adobe.com/email/

[21] Alex Moore. "7 Tips for Getting More Responses to Your Emails (With Data!). *Boomerang.* February 12, 2016. http://blog.boomerangapp.com/2016/02/7-tips-for-getting-more-responses-to-your-emails-with-data/

[22] Camille L. Ryan and Kurt Bauman. "Educational Attainment in the United States: 2015." *U.S. Census Bureau.* March 2016. https://www.census.gov/content/dam/Census/library/publications/2016/demo/p20-578.pdf

[23] Camille L. Ryan and Kurt Bauman. "Educational Attainment in the United States: 2015." *U.S. Census Bureau.* March 2016. https://www.census.gov/content/dam/Census/library/publications/2016/demo/p20-578.pdf

[24] Upland Adestra. "Top 10 Email Clients in March 2019." 2020. https://uplandsoftware.com/adestra/resources/blog/top-10-email-clients/

[25] Kristin Naragon. "Subject: Email, We Just Can't Get Enough." Adobe Blog. August 26, 2015. https://theblog.adobe.com/email/

[26] Amreen Bhujwala. "6 Ways to Use Personalization in Email Subject Lines for Better Open Rates." *Constant Contact.* January 2020. https://blogs.constantcontact.com/personalization-in-email-subject-lines/

[27] Alex Moore. "7 Tips for Getting More Responses to Your Emails (With Data!). *Boomerang.* February 12, 2016. http://blog.boomerangapp.com/2016/02/7-tips-for-getting-more-responses-to-your-emails-with-data/

[28] Brendan G. "How to Start an Email: An Email Openings Analysis of 300,000+ Messages." *Boomerang.* December 14, 2017. https://blog.boomerangapp.com/2017/12/how-to-start-an-email-an-email-openings-analysis/

[29] Brendan G. "How to Start an Email: An Email Openings Analysis of 300,000+ Messages." *Boomerang.* December 14, 2017. https://blog.boomerangapp.com/2017/12/how-to-start-an-email-an-email-openings-analysis/

[30] Kristin Naragon. "Subject: Email, We Just Can't Get Enough." Adobe Blog. August 26, 2015. https://theblog.adobe.com/email/

[31] Upland Adestra. "Top 10 Email Clients in March 2019." 2020. https://uplandsoftware.com/adestra/resources/blog/top-10-email-clients/

ACKNOWLEDGEMENTS

Many thanks to my two fantastic children, Zack and Alexa, for your patience with me to finish this book. Thank you for giving me the quiet time I needed to work at my laptop!

Wonderful thanks to my awesome family, for their love and support—my mother, Audree Peters; my older brother Jeff, and his wife Misty Peters; and my younger brother Joe, and his wife Christine Peters. You all have been my biggest "fan club" over the years. I really appreciate you!

Also, to my "extended family"—Adrienne Cavarly, Ann and Gary Harvey, Rich and Peggy Humrichouse. I am very grateful for your help and support, especially during this past year...which turned out to be MUCH more challenging than any of us ever expected!

Special thanks go to my fantastic friends Michelle Schwartz, Jeannette Wolpink, Melissa DellaPenna, Jenny Zygmunt, Ann Callow, and Steve Kolb for our regular chats during the creation of this book concept—as well as for your endless support, encouragement, and listening ears for all my new ideas this year for my business, Peters Writing Services, and for this book.

Also, to my excellent dinner club group—Brenda and Scott

Perrea, Aunie and Marty Perrea, Michelle and Dugger Schwartz, Jennifer and Adam Elliott, and Ryan Humrichouse. You encouraged me to complete this book at our various get-togethers, especially this past Christmas—when the finish line looked VERY far away!

Brittany Lynn, I'm so grateful to you for being my role-model and mentor over the years. And I appreciate our continued friendship with you, Benjy, and Henry!

Scott Meyer, thank you for believing in me and encouraging me. Without all of your "extra help" for me, the kids, and the house this year, I could not have finished this book!

Karla Snider, thank you so much for your awesome design skills...you have helped me and my business in so many ways over the past 18 years. And Mark Short, I'm very grateful to you for your expertise and patience answering my 1,001 questions about my website and growing my distribution list.

...And I hope that my way-cool dad, Dick Peters (4th grade teacher extraordinaire), who passed away 12 years ago, would have enjoyed this book too. I miss you!

ABOUT THE AUTHOR

Paula Peters

Paula Peters is an award-winning technical writer who has trained more than 10,000 executives, military officers, government officials, and entrepreneurs on today's current writing standards. She has published 4 books, including The Quick-and-Easy Website and The Ultimate Marketing Toolkit, and 450+ articles on writing, business, and web content. As President of Peters Writing Services, Inc. for the past 21 years, she has written everything from audit manuals to annual reports to web content for a wide variety of organizations across the globe—such as the U.S. Army, Russell Stover, U.S. Strategic Command, Broadway, Red Robin, Bank of the West, Sprint, Applebee's, U.S. Cyber Command, the EPA, and more. She lives and works in Kansas City with her two children, Zack and Alexa. Learn more at: www.peterswriting.com.

BOOKS BY THIS AUTHOR

The Ultimate Marketing Toolkit

From e-mail to YouTube, Facebook to webvertising—the tools of marketing have never changed so quickly. Now marketing professionals can ensure their business has the best marketing plan, supported by the most cutting-edge techniques. This book gives marketers what they need to make their businesses thrive. In simple, nontechnical language, Paula Peters shows professionals how to use marketing tools like:

Blogs and blogging
Pay-per-click advertising
Search engine optimization
E-mail offers
E-newsletters

Filled with samples and resource lists, this book is the only book a marketing professional will ever need.

The Quick-And-Easy Web Site

Forget the complicated instructions and baffling techspeak found in other guides, The Quick-and-Easy Web Site gives you straightforward instruction on how to build a Web page that really delivers. It's simple. It's fast. And it's certain to take your small business to the next level.

Written for the small-business owner on the go, this book gets your Web site up and running in just one day. It walks you through the five easy steps that will get your company the Internet attention it deserves. Learn how to:

Purchase your domain name
Write powerful Web content
Design your page's layout
Find a Web host
Publish your site

Once your new site goes active, you'll attract new customers in no time. This fast and effective guide puts you and your company where you belong-on the Web!

Working Mom's Survival Guide

More women than ever before are going back to work soon after having a baby. And no matter what their job, making the transition from home to work can be really challenging. Whether dealing with day-to-day dilemmas like spitup on their power suits or big-picture problems like the cost of child care, new moms need relief! Written in a friendly and encouraging tone, this guide is all a stressed-out mother needs to organize her life so everyone's happy—including herself! From prebaby planning to after-baby adjustments, this book covers it all, including:

FMLA and maternity leave
Temporary schedules and career planning
Job changes
Child care
Responsibilities at home
Caring for yourself
Considering a new job
Choosing to quit
Dealing with unexpected or special challenges

With this book by their side, new mothers can have their careers—and be great moms, too!

Made in the USA
Middletown, DE
07 February 2024